First Foods to Family Meals

Help Your Child To Prepare and Enjoy Food With Your Family

Sarah Moudry

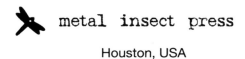
metal insect press

Houston, USA

Use of the tools and appliances referenced in this book for the purpose of cooking and baking involve inherent risk. The author takes no responsibility for the reader's actions. Furthermore, no part of this book is a substitute for the professional advice of a physician, dietitian, or allergist. The reader should consult with these professionals before making and serving any foods described in this book.

Acknowledgements

This book would not be possible without the guidance, inspiration, contributions, and experience of so many. Thank you to my friends, and friends of friends. Thank you to those who reviewed the recipes: Roelie Hartwig, Jo Howell, Mary Pfiefer, Ben Preston, and Megan Tyne.

Thank you to all of the parents and children who have cooked with me at Studio June, to those who have shopped with me at the market, and to my own children for showing me the possibilities for collaborative work.

Thank you to my family members who have contributed to and supported my love of cooking and my appreciation of family meals:

My Grandma Krug,was a professional cook and a master in her own farmhouse kitchen. She always had something cooking. I remember watching her hustle from stove to kitchen table, with serving bowl after serving bowl. Some of my first memories of cooking are by her side, in a hairnet, at the Gailey Eye Clinic. Your passion to provide nourishment to so many has inspired me to provide for others.

My mother always has a recipe book open on her counter. As children, she included my sisters and me in the kitchen and was always willing to try a new recipe. She never hid the vegetables and always helped connect us to the ingredients in a recipe, whether it was the blueberries from our garden in Grand Rapids or the fresh seafood from the market in Pittsburgh. Your adventurous spirit and willingness to try new recipes has helped me create a space for this with my own family.

My father taught me the joy that can come from sharing a meal. When I was younger, in that family of five, I remember our quiet family meals at home. As our family has filled with three sons-in-law and eight grandchildren, you continue to host us in your house and at your favorite restaurants. I have watched you share with my own children the joy of a two-hour meal at a restaurant. Hours of ordering, talking, tasting, and laughing. I cannot thank you enough for sharing with me the feelings of family and connection that are communicated through a shared meal.

My husband James is my forever support. Whatever idea I have, you are right there to listen and support me in any way to get it from concept to creation. Whether it's a cake or a new business, I can depend on you. Each meal we prepare for our family is a reminder of your support and confidence in me.

Contents

First Foods to Family Meals

x

— Part I —
Introduction

"Once I tune into the fact that my family receives my cooking for them as an act of love - that it's actually something that makes them feel cared for — it shifts my entire perspective."

— Joanna Gaines

My Perspective

"Cooking is all about people. Food is maybe the only universal thing that really has the power to bring everyone together. No matter what culture, everywhere around the world, people get together to eat."

— Guy Fieri

Preparing, sharing, and eating food are daily activities for most people. An experience that connects us all. Eating involves many different senses, preparing food is linked with distinct memories, and sharing food is connected with relationships.

So many memories are often tied to food. Whether it is preparing, gathering, discussing, planning, or eating, food is a part of our daily experience. Food is a necessity to life. It is a source of great pleasure for some and great pain for others. Some eat just to restore energy and don't think much about emotion that may be tied to the experience.

Certain foods and their smells can bring back vivid memories of childhood and loved ones. You may remember cookies your grandma made, stirring pudding with your mom that took so long to cook on the stove and needed constant attention, or even watching through the window of the oven door as a loaf of bread rose and became golden brown. Participating in cooking is a way we connect with food and understand its simplicity as well as complexity. When we practice cooking, we learn how to bring out the bright green color in broccoli. Experience in preparing food teaches us how to wash mushrooms without them absorbing the water like sponges. Trial and error is often how we learn about the chemistry in baking and the delicate balance between sugar and yeast.

Food preparation is not the only way we develop human connections through food. Serving a meal or hosting a party are other ways. My own memories of food include large family dinners, extended family gatherings, and even a very rare meal in front of the television.

For some, their relationship with food is a painful one—a constant internal conversation about will-power and abstention. If you have developed challenging emotions around food, it will take an intentional effort to help your child have his own relationship with food that is not overpowered by your own discomfort with over- or under-eating.

Parents can also have food aversions they must be conscious to not pass on. Whether it was a single experience with food poisoning, or a repeated discomfort with a particular food texture, your child witnesses and may repeat the attitude you express toward food. This doesn't mean you have to love and eat every food. However, it will help your child develop his own opinions if you do not express displeasure or disgust with food.

A child develops his attitude about preparing, eating, and sharing food from his environment, including the interactions with adults in that environment. This means that the attitudes that surround him on a daily basis help him form his own beliefs. This starts from birth and is strongest in his first three years of life. It is in these years that he takes in what is around him without censorship or opinion. He doesn't yet have belief about what is right or wrong. He is learning from everyone in his environment. He sees what exists around him.

This formative time is significant as a child develops an adventurous attitude about trying new foods, a willingness to participate in preparing food, and a connection to his family through shared meals. This is the time when a child might either develop a picky attitude or broader attitude about his preferred diet.

Babies come into the world ready to nurse. Within a year, they are sitting at the dinner table and sharing in the family meal. It takes twelve months to go from suckling milk to seated and chewing a full range of foods.

How does this happen? How does a child make this transition? How can parents best support this transition? How can parents help their child develop healthy attitudes about food and healthy eating habits from the start?

These are the first questions to ask. We will answer these in the following pages and then move on to tackle the topics of family meals, baking with your child, and then fostering independence in the kitchen.

After completing my second level of Montessori teacher training, my husband and I had our first child. As a new parent, I used this training to make so many parenting choices that I decided that I would focus on sharing these methods with other parents. I offer this book as a parent and educator. I have written this book with the hope of supporting other families who want to empower their child through gaining skills in the kitchen and strengthen their family bond through collaborative work. I am not a physician nor a nutritionist. In many ways, I am simply a mom. A mom sharing with other moms (and dads, and grandparents, and caregivers.) I have a story to tell about what I have learned in my work with families and I want to share it so others have the tools they need for intentional parenting practices.

This book describes how using the Montessori philosophy can support your goals to foster independence in your child, support your child's natural desire to explore, and set limits that are reasonable for parents and developmentally appropriate for children.

The activities and suggestions in this book come from my Montessori training, experiences with my own three children, and the many other children and parents I have had the honor of working with over the years. As I have written this book, I have tried to include each of them by using rotating pronouns. When you read this book, I hope you can find a connection for your own experience. Whether you read she, he, or they, my hope is that I have communicated that all children and parents are included in this view of connecting through food.

A Note on Language

I use the phrase "young children" to describe children who are between one and three years old and are new to walking instead of calling them "toddlers." The word toddler names the age group for how they move, which we do not do with other ages.

What Is Montessori?

"The environment must be rich in motives which lend interest to activity and invite the child to conduct his own activity."

— Maria Montessori

It is not difficult to come across the word Montessori if you have children. It is all over the Internet, in school names, and in many books about child development. The Montessori education method is named for Maria Montessori. Montessori was an Italian Doctor who developed an innovative educational system and approach in the early 20th Century. Montessori then introduced her scientific pedagogy all over the world. Her method is used explicitly in over 20,000 schools around the world and it influences many times that number. It also influences many families. Parents looking to support their children's natural development incorporate Montessori philosophy into their homes and raise their children with these principles incorporated in their parenting choices.

Montessori philosophy defines a few clear principles that help us to determine the choices that are best for our children, ourselves, and our families. These basic ideas are: *offering choice, experience with reality, independence, responsiveness, and being child-centered.*

1. Choice

Allowing for choice helps empower the individual. When a young child chooses between two options he is connected with the decisions within the family. He understands that his input is valued and therefore he is a valued member of the family. If all choices are made *for* a young child, he can feel as if life just happens around him and he is not an active participant. These early opportunities for choice help him to build and exercise his will in a meaningful way. This practice is responsible for later independent decision making. The opportunity to collaborate from a young age prepares an older child to evaluate choices, anticipate potential consequences, and then make their choices.

Making choices also allows a child to experience failure. These moments of choosing, failing, and recovering help children understand the impact of their choices. It also helps them to build confidence as they learn and improve their skills. This is one of the most important attributes they will learn in their early years—self-efficacy.

2. Reality-Based

Starting at birth and continuing through maturity, it is important to offer real things and experiences first. The understanding of what is possible and what can be imagined and created is based in the knowledge of what is real. Children's understanding of reality provides the later springboard into imagination and creativity. If a child is given the imaginary first, they simply recreate or mimic what is given to them. However, if they are first given reality, they reflect that reality. They show us their understanding of the world. As that understanding grows, forming a strong foundation, they grow to show us what their own imagination is capable of. Understanding what is *real* allows children to imagine what could be.

Real experiences require a child to touch, feel, taste, smell, and hear their environment. These experiences connect their sensorial learning to their intellect. The work they do with their hands and body feeds their intellectual development and expands their understanding of the world. Pulling a carrot from the ground in the garden informs the senses in a way that only the physical experience can. There is no replacement for such real experiences.

In my own children, I have seen this in their storytelling, playwriting, and engineering capabilities. They understand the reality of the present, and then they think out-of-the-box to imagine new possibilities. Out-of-the-box thinking starts by understanding the boundaries of the box.

3. Independence

From even the first days of life, a child is honored as their own being. Children are not owned by nor are they an extension of their parents, but are each their own individual person. This is important to recognize when taking a Montessori approach; this view frames how you will see your child's actions and how you will set limits, offer opportunities, and interact with your child. When you begin with the idea that your child is separate from you and has his own life path, you recognize that you may offer choices in his life and he may choose differently than you. He may respond in a different way and he will have a different personality than you. He is similar to you, and he is his own, separate person.

Once we see our child as a separate person, we can see all the ways he can function independently. We can offer developmentally appropriate opportunities as he grows that help him to actualize his own capabilities. When he is an infant, he cannot dress himself, yet we can talk to him during his diaper change, naming his left leg and right leg as he gets a clean diaper. We do this knowing his receptive language is developing and, with consistency, he will soon learn to participate in diaper changes.

For older children, supporting the development of independence allows him to participate in family life in a real way. He can carry groceries and he can help choose recipes for dinner. When we include our children in these activities, we empower them to have independent thought and then, by following through, we show that we value their input.

When a child learns to be physically independent he learns to respond to and satisfy his own needs. He feels the confidence that develops with these skills and he sees what more he can do in his life. He starts to develop independent thought and ideas. An independent thinker is creative, thinks outside-the-box, and is innovative. A person who expects ingenuity from himself sees how he can connect to his community and contribute. He sees his value as an individual. Understanding his own value, he sees and values the contributions of others. All of this is the foundation of community.

Supporting a child's developing independence, both physical and intellectual, takes love and patience from parents. There are days when you will see great strides, and other days when you question your choice to support your child's development in this way. This is not exclusive to choosing to incorporate Montessori in your parenting. All parents, no matter their methods or philosophy have these moments. It is because you love them deeply that you want the best for them, and it is because life is ever-changing that you question your choices. Patience and trust in your child's development are the keys.

4. Responsive

In Montessori, *responsive* refers to the environment and the people. Montessori determined her method of education by observing children and then responding by either changing her interaction with the children or by changing something in the environment. Her choices were based on the needs, actions, and interactions she observed in the children.

We know from Montessori's work that if we step back and watch carefully, without assumption or judgement, we are more likely to see the true intention behind a child's actions. Seeing this allows us to provide meaningful opportunity. If we see that a child keeps going to the same cabinet and pulling out all of the pots and pans, the child has a need to explore. If we are frustrated and want to stop this behavior we can: lock the cabinet so the child stops getting into the pots and pans; or replace the pots and pans with something we are ok with the child exploring (containers with lids) in the cabinet. In this way, we allow the environment to set the limit and the child can regulate his movements based on the opportunity.

Similarly, an infant may throw his food off his plate and onto the floor. Many parents struggle with this stage in development and find themselves saying, "no" and possibly even shouting. This moment of frustration can be mitigated by understanding that the child is *testing*. He may be testing the concept of gravity, the interest in a pet to eat his food, or even your patience. Whichever it is, he is testing. The parent can: remove the food and offer it later when the child is obviously hungry; or remove the interesting part of the experience that the child is looking for whether it's the family dog, or your frustrated reaction (removal of gravity is likely not a preferred option). By making these changes, the parent defines the limits of the environment and removes the need for correcting the child. Children will find the limit within the environment and choose a different action.

5. Child-Centered

This can be a complex concept to follow within a family home. In a Montessori school, this makes perfect sense to have the classrooms child-centered. In a family home, we want to have a home that supports each person in the family, not just the child. We can create child-centered areas within each room in the home. In the kitchen, this means having access to child-size tools and opportunities to prepare food independently and collaboratively. This does not mean that every recipe includes child involvement, but it does mean that with a little preparation, there are opportunities for children to participate.

When we create child-centered spaces, we send a message to our children that they are a welcome member of the family. By creating some areas of the house to be child-centered such as the bathroom and the kitchen, but not others, like the parent's bedroom, we send the message that there are spaces that are prepared for children, and there are other spaces that are not. Limits like this are helpful for children. When they can see clearly the limits, and parents consistently follow through with communicating these limits, children are able to self-regulate.

Child-centered spaces support children's development of choice, their movement, their intellect, their will, and independence. A child learns how to care for himself and others by having accessible tools and activities. Child-centered spaces allow parents to step back and allow their child to develop naturally. These spaces require a parent to spend some time preparing and maintaining the space, but in time, they allow a parent the freedom to step back and not have to do for their child.

For example, when your house has a low bench with a basket for shoes and a low hook for a coat just inside the door, you can show your child how to use the space. With consistent practice, your child learns to use this space independently. Once a child is using this space independently, getting ready to leave the house requires that a parent say. "Get your shoes on. It's time to go." There is no need to put a child's shoes on for him.

Montessori philosophy is complex and has more concepts and points than just the five principles I have defined here. However, as a parent, following these five principles will help you develop your own respectful and intentional parenting style.

Cycle of Activity

In Montessori practice, it is important to honor the beginning, middle and end of each activity. Helping a child move through the complete cycle allows him to see the steps that lead to completion. The feeling of completion creates joy, confidence, and independence.

In order for a child to understand each of the activities in his life, it is best to give time separately to each of them. Eating is an activity, sleeping is an activity, a diaper change is an activity, and playing is an activity. Focussing on the activity at hand keeps parents present in the moment with their child. Experiencing this moment together gives your child knowledge of the activity and eventually will lead to their ownership of repeating those activities independently.

Considering again the example of the diaper change, saying to your child, "I'm lifting your left leg." As you do lift their left leg helps them connect the feeling and the words. If you are distracted and talking on the phone, the language they hear from you is not connected with their experience. Staying in the moment will allow them to participate once they are capable of lifting a leg; becoming an active participant in their own care.

Starting in infancy, you help set the pattern of being present in each activity. Then, as your child grows and becomes mobile, you can continue to build on this foundation. You create habits of completing each activity before moving on the the next. Supporting your child to engage in one activity at a time helps develop important skills they will need throughout life.

Concentration - A child develops concentration through opportunities to complete an activity, uninterrupted. Interruption to concentration keeps one from actualizing their potential. Concentration allows one to repeat and practice in order to develop and perfect skills.

Self-Awareness - Understanding the task he is doing brings self-awareness. Knowing where one is in the process of a task and what one needs to complete the task, supports a broader understanding of how things work, how things get done, and what is needed to move on to the next task.

Coordinated Movement - This growth is needed in order to independently complete tasks. A child needs to be able to pick up a fork and get it to his mouth in order to feed himself. If this activity is interrupted by running around the house during a meal, or interfered with by an adult feeding him while he watches a screen, he may take longer to develop the strong hands and coordination for this activity. These hand and coordination skills will be needed all throughout his life. He will need strong hands for writing, for building, and for creating. Using tools is not isolated to eating. If a child is intellectually ready for an activity, but not physically ready, he can be frustrated and held hostage by his own lack of coordination and dexterity. Allowing your child to develop basic feeding skills without interruption, allows him to prepare himself for his next developmental stage.

Self-Direction - When one has an understanding of what is required of a particular activity, one can choose that activity with intention. If a child feels hunger, he can choose to eat. If he doesn't understand that the discomfort he is feeling is hunger, he cannot choose to ease the feeling. He may then resort to tantrums because he does not understand. A child begins to understand the connection between activity and the feeling by doing one activity at a time. When we help a child do one activity at a time, we help him connect the activity to the feelings associated with that activity. When a child is allowed to watch a video in order to distract him from the task of sitting and eating, he may not develop the awareness needed to eat with intention. In this situation, the eating is almost hidden. Taking the time to eat, enjoy food, enjoy company, and acknowledge that your body needs nourishment is an important part of understanding your own body and how to take care of it.

Respects Limits - When you stop a child from doing multiple activities at one time you set a limit. You create a rule that he can rely on. Children need (and like) clear rules. To quote Brené Brown, "Clear is kind. Unclear is unkind." (Dare to Lead by Brené Brown) This doesn't mean that children won't test the rules. Testing is a way for a child to show that he knows there is a rule and he is checking to make sure you will consistently enforce the rule. Setting the limit with activities helps to maintain clear guidelines about expectations in your home.

The Beginnings

"Sharing food with another human being is an intimate act
that should not be indulged in lightly."

— *M.F.K. Fisher*

Food is a necessity. On a basic level, we need food to live. Healthful eating supports healthy body and brain development. Food however is also a sensory and social experience. For this reason, the relationship between a child and parent will set the foundation of how a child approaches and enjoys food. Different personalities have different perspectives on food. Some people savor every bite. Others take it in as quickly as possible just to get through it, while still others can forget to eat until they are famished. These styles can be visible even in an infants first feedings. Considering that your child is taking in everything around him and watching others in his environment, your own relationship with food can become a part of our child's connection with food. In order for your child to learn to respond to feelings of hunger and fullness, to continue to try new foods, and to form his own opinions about food, it helps to keep a few things in mind.

- Understand your own experiences, preferences, and biases about food. Once your child is eating solid food, try not to judge their choices on taste, texture, and combinations of foods.

- Set a good example for eating balanced meals.

- Let go of expectations of how much your child eats. Once you are offering solid food, as long as the food you offer is always healthful, your child will find the right amount to eat.

The first feedings can set the stage for connecting a feeling of love and care with food. When a child is born, one of the first questions that a parent answers is, "Will we breastfeed, formula feed, or offer a combination?" Many parents try to determine this before baby is born. There are breastfeeding classes, bottle feeding classes, classes for learning to pump. There are so many options while you are pregnant. The truth is, the feeding relationship cannot actually be defined until the parent and infant meet. Additionally, parents who adopt or participate in surrogacy may not have the same options. It is wonderful to study before your baby arrives, and it can help ease stress to stay open to the idea that your feeding relationship with your child may take time. From my own experience, each of my three babies had a different feeding relationship with me. Each of my babies had their own process of learning to suck and how to signal when they were hungry and when they were finished.

When a newborn is held in arms for a feeding he rests about 12 inches from the face of the person feeding him. This is also the distance he can see at birth. As you hold him and he eats, it is important to make eye contact. The activity of the moment is connection. Many parents can feel that they are not needed in that moment and while holding the bottle or nursing, they open an article or an email on their phone and they start to read. Doing these things interferes with the connection between parent and child. Your infant needs your full attention. Show him you are there with him in that moment. Show him that your relationship is based on connection and sharing experience. Watch him as he eats. Learn his facial expressions and movements. Take this time to tell him a story, sing to him, or sit together peacefully.

Whether breastfeeding or bottle feeding (with breastmilk or formula), the feeding times are about more than just nutrition. Offering and receiving food are tied to the feeling of connection and love, for both parent and infant. The space you prepare for feeding and your conscious presence during feedings are key in nurturing your relationship.

- Create a space to feed - Find a chair that is comfortable that does not have distracting screens or extra noise nearby. As often as possible, feed in this chair. Your baby will find the consistency comforting and will develop points of reference in this space. He will learn that when he is in this space it is time to eat.

- Keep the mood calm - Keep the feeding time free of phones, other personal digital devices, and digital screens. Setup a low-light environment as your baby's eyes are sensitive.

- Connect - Look your baby in the eyes and talk or sing to her. Be present; sit quietly together, learning each other's body language and facial expressions.

- Keep baby awake - feeding is an active and comforting activity. Newborns often fall asleep while feeding. Keeping your baby awake while feeding maintains eating as its own activity, not a means to fall asleep. To keep your baby awake during feedings, talk to him, or rub his feet. You may also uncover him a bit to keep him from getting too warm. A baby may become drowsy while eating and then can be put in his bed to sleep. However, it is best to not let him fall into a deep sleep while feeding. Following this guideline will help him learn to self-soothe to fall asleep independently and helps to set the foundation of eating as its own activity.

In the beginning, parents create the positive experiences with food through the feedings that happen during the day and through the night. When a newborn is hungry, he cries out for food. When a parent responds to this cry with warm milk, an infant feels satisfied and that he is loved as his needs are met. This continues through the first months of life and your baby learns that when he calls for food, he will be satisfied. His trust in his parents and in the world builds. This basic trust is the start of your infant's feelings of security as he grows more aware of his surroundings. As new people interact with him and as you introduce him to new places, he will rely on this foundation of basic trust, established in his first months, to feel secure and allow himself to connect socially. Food and comfort are connected. Food and trust are connected.

This is important even through the night. One of the most difficult times to be present with your baby is when you are over-tired. In the middle of the night, the emotional connection that happens during a feeding is just as important as those that happen throughout the day. These feedings can be shared between parents.

Some families may choose to ask a grandparent or another close relative to help with feedings. Many family members are often excited to help in this way. If you choose to have support for feedings, prepare your chosen family member with the importance to make eye contact, be present, and keep the mood calm during feedings.

As he grows, your baby's feedings become more efficient and therefore shorter and less frequent. He is more aware and active during feedings. Find a quiet place for feeding him. As he becomes more aware of the world he will be distracted by what is around him and pull away to watch. This can become frustrating for both parent and child, as the parent wants efficiency and the child is hungry but wants to watch.

The first six months of feedings are all one-on-one interactions. You hold your child in your arms and offer him his milk meals. At this point, it can be difficult to imagine how your infant will go from this cradled position, to sitting at a table and chewing solid food. It is a gradual transition that will start about his sixth month.

Food Allergies
If you have concerns or questions about food allergies,
talk with your pediatrician before introducing any solid foods.

Weaning

As your baby nears six months old, you will notice some changes that signal he is getting ready to start solid foods. The transition to solid food—weaning—is a process that will slowly happen over the next six months.

Eating solid food requires learning new skills. He will start to learn to bite and chew for nutrition rather than suck. He will learn to use his tongue to move and hold food and his hands to pick up and deliver food to his mouth. Rather than being held to eat, he will learn to sit across from you. He will become independent in his ability to satisfy his need for food.

Signs your child is ready to start solid food

• <u>Notices food</u>: Around age five-and-a-half to six months, you may notice your child start to watch when you are eating. She will watch you move food from your plate to your mouth and may even grab at food if you have her in your lap. This is a a signal that she is getting ready to start solid food. Noticing and following your child's interest when it is developmentally appropriate is what Maria Montessori described as "following the child". This is an important concept in Montessori education. To follow the child, an adult recognizes a child's natural interest in something and supports the natural development of the skills needed to satisfy that interest. See the Montessori principle "Responsive" on page 10 and "Follow the Child on page 24 for more details.

• <u>Sitting well</u>: Another sign that a child is ready to start solid foods is his strong, straight back when he is sitting independently. He is developing strong core muscles and can now hold himself in the sitting position for a meal. The sitting position is important to help create good eating habits and minimize the risk of choking. When a child is sitting independently, he can sit in a low, sturdy chair at a weaning table.

• <u>Hand skills</u>: Your child is starting to use his hands to pick things up, move objects from hand-to-hand, and holding objects and putting them in his mouth. He may even be starting to pick things up with just his fingers. These are skills he needs for self-feeding and will strengthen with the introduction of solid food and practice. You can introduce flatware, an open cup, plates, and bowls from his first meal. This is the time for him to learn. Children who are not given the opportunity to participate in self-feeding from their first solid-food meals, may push back on self-feeding later and it can become a burden on both parent and child to hand-feed a two- or three-year-old child.

• <u>Emergence of teeth</u>: The age at which first teeth come in can vary. However, even before the teeth come in, children often begin salivating quite a bit and rubbing their gums. Their jaws are strong and while teeth will help to break up food, they are not essential. With time, as a child gets more teeth he will learn to use them in combination with his strong jaws, for chewing.

The First Weaning Meal

The first weaning meal is given at the weaning table and chair with a real set of dishes.. Here, for the first time, you can sit across from your child to feed him. Your relationship is changing as you sit with him ready for some conversation and supporting his independence as he is ready.

A step-by-step guide:

1. Choose a time of day that is not hectic. It will be important for both you and your child to be present in the moment and not distracted by other activities in the house. The solid food meal you are introducing is intended to eventually replace a liquid meal, so make sure to offer this meal at a time your child would usually eat.

2. Prepare the solid food you intend to feed your child so that is it fresh, but not hot. Bring a tray with a serving size of the food in a bowl, a small pitcher with water, and a couple damp cloths to the are when you will feed your child, but not on the weaning table.

3. Set the table with the placemat and real dishes. He doesn't yet know how to handle all these tools, but with time and opportunity he will learn to feed himself and the right use for each tool. It is important for him to see the simple table setting layout consistently at each meal. He then internalizes the order and will learn to keep the physical order. If you find the dishes distracting to him during the meal, you can slide the setting away from him, just out of reach. This can help for some children and is a temporary situation; it is important to consider each meal a new opportunity and give him the chance to manage the dishes in front of him. If you

Weaning Table and Chair

A weaning table and chair are designed for the stature and coordination of a baby between six months and one-and-half years. Low, sturdy, and easily wipeable, your child can use this set for his first meals and many beyond. The chair has sides so that he will not tip out, and he feels secure while at the table.

The weaning table and chair are usually heavier than a typical child's table and chair. This is to keep a sturdy and solid base for young children who are still a bit wobbly. This table and chair is used for any meal that your child may be eating alone, or just with one other person. When the family eats together, children will sit at the family table in chairs that bring them up to share the same table surface as the family. A high chair with tray should not be used. Standard high chairs work well if the tray is removed so your child eats from the same surface as others in the family. A more desirable high chair is one that supports his posture, allows his feet to be flat, not dangle, and the height can be adjusted as he grows taller. These chairs often are designed for a child's growing independence, and later for getting in and out of the chair on his own. (See page 52 for more on high chairs.)

find he is still distracted by the dishes, gently say to him, "I see these dishes are distracting you from eating. I will slide them over here so you can focus on eating."

4. Introduce the table and set-up to your child by naming each item. His receptive language is quite large and babies love hearing the names of the things in their environment.

5. With your child in his weaning chair, sit across from him and put a small amount of the food on a spoon and place the spoon on the plate in front of him. Offer a small bite of the food you have prepared, e.g., puréed sweet potato, on a separate spoon. As he works to try to pick-up the spoon on the plate, you keep offering small amounts of food. At first, he may not know how to chew or may scrunch his nose or turn away from the

food. It is all very different from nursing or a bottle and he will need time to get used to textures, flavors, and using his mouth in a new way. When he is done eating, he will turn away or let you know by fussing.

6. Offer the glass with a small amount of water after every few bites of food. You will judge how much water and when your child needs to drink. Now that your child is eating solid food, he will need water at each meal. At first, he will need your help to hold the glass while he learns to sip. After a couple days of practice, you can help him hold the glass in his two hands. He may then start to pick it up on his own. Holding the glass is easier than putting it back down; help to guide his hands back to the table. Repeated practice using the dishes and tools will allow him the trust in the routine, the opportunity to practice, and the experience with new foods and textures.

7. When he is finished, offer him a wet cloth to hold while you wipe his hands and face with another. Always invite him to take part in his own self-care.

8. Remove your child from the weaning table, find a comfortable place to sit together and finish the meal with nursing or a bottle. Your baby's first solid-food meals may be only a few bites and last only five minutes. At the end of each meal, offer his regular milk or formula. When he first starts solid foods, he may tire of eating before he is actually full. Finishing the meal with breastfeeding or a bottle allows him to complete his meal and maintain his nutrition until he is able to eat enough solid food in one sitting to provide the needed nutrition.

Once you introduce a food, offer it three to five days in a row. This will give your child time to get used to the taste and texture and give you time to notice any possible reactions to the food.

A Well-Balanced Meal

Each liquid meal of breast milk or formula that you feed your baby is a complete meal. It contains healthy fats, vitamins, minerals, protein, and carbohydrates. At about seven months, you have introduced many different new

Skip the Sippy Cup

Children who can use two hands to hold an object are ready to hold a small glass and drink from it. Only put a little water or milk in the cup at a time. It will take practice to master this skill. An open glass is a better choice for your child's development than the common "sippy cup". We never used "sippy cups" with our children and never felt the need to. When we were on the go, we would take a water bottle if we needed a way to carry a drink with us.

A child's mouth, tongue, and throat are developing and at around one-year old. His swallow pattern needs to evolve and mature to strengthen, prepare to take in solid food, and develop spoken language skills. When a child uses a "sippy cup" the spout blocks the tongue from elevating during drinking which can interfere with the development of spoken language.

Additionally, the "sippy cup" was designed for the convenience of adults. It prevents spills. If a child is seated and drinking from a cup, he may spill. It happens. Spilling gives him real feedback about physical properties and interactions of the world. As mentioned earlier, it is important to set clear expectations for eating and drinking. A child should not be allowed to walk around with a drink. If he wants to move, put the cup away. If he wants to drink, ask him to sit at the table. This limits spills in areas that are difficult to clean.

foods to your child, he is eating more at each sitting, and he is ready to fully replace one liquid meal with a full solid food meal. Each solid food meal you offer should also be a complete meal. A single serving of banana does not replace a liquid meal. Some banana mash is only part of a complete meal that is offered.

Example — A Balanced Meal

• Egg yolk (hard boiled and mashed, mixed with some breastmilk or formula)

• Puréed sweet potato (roasted with olive oil)

• Mashed banana with infant cereal

• Water

Introducing Finger Foods

Between seven and nine months you can introduce your child to chunkier textures and finger foods. Offering small, soft pieces of legumes, fruits, and vegetables can hold his interest in eating while expanding his experience with texture and chewing.

It is important not to stay with purées any longer than needed. A child who is served purées for more than a couple of months, may start to prefer only puréed foods and not learn the skills needed to chew and swallow. By nine months, your child can generally move to two solid food meals a day and then to three meals a day by twelve months. Three meals a day and a couple of small snacks in between is enough nutrition to completely wean your child from the breast or bottle between twelve and fourteen months.

Milk can now be taken from a glass and water is served at every meal. Families have many options on types of milk. Some families may prefer a plant-based milk while others choose an animal milk.

In the United States, the American Academy of Pediatrics (AAP) currently recommends[1]:

• Infants should be exclusively breastfed for the first six months.

• After the first six months, an infant should be gradually introduced to solid food until one year old.

• After one year of age, breastfeeding can be completed or continued if mutually desired by the mother and infant.

Some of the nursing moms with whom I have worked feel that around one-year old is a natural time to complete weaning, while others feel this is too soon. If you have access to fresh fruits, vegetables, healthful proteins, and clean drinking water, nutritionally, your child is ready to complete her weaning. Choosing whether to continue the nursing relationship beyond this age is an emotional decision. As a parent, your choice to support their independence also includes their emotional and social independence. You help them to learn new ways of soothing themselves, and interacting with you to support this development. A child who has coping skills, such as taking a deep breath when frustrated, can employ those skills in stressful moments. A nursing child without such skills may look to find his mother to nurse to calm down. If you are in the process of ceasing your nursing relationship (weaning) and your child comes to you for soothing, offer a warm embrace, communicate your confidence in their ability to calm themselves, and offer a bonding opportunity such as singing a song or reading a book together. In moments like this I remember helping each of my children to sit with me and take three deep breaths together.

This skill building can start about the time your child is crawling. This does not mean this is when you stop nursing. This means, you can be mindful of when your child is nursing for nutrition and when they are nursing for comfort. If they are coming to you for comfort, you can introduce new ways to cope. Completing the nursing relationship while balancing with skill building is a process, and one your child can be ready for by twelve to fourteen months.

Follow The Child

Montessori teachers and parents often us the phrase, "Follow the Child." Following the child is not as simple as letting a child do whatever he wants. It means to recognize the need and then respond with the appropriate activity, always with developmentally appropriate limits.

If a child new to sitting and eating solid food throws a fork, it is best to replace the fork on the table and then show him again how to use it. If he throws the fork again, this is probably a sign he is not hungry, or at least more interested in throwing than eating. Remove the food and offer it again later, rather than allow him to throw the utensils. You may want to take him to a space with a basket of balls and invite him to throw the balls. As he displays the need to throw, we can show him an item that is appropriate to throw and do not allow the misuse of a tool. This is done with love and care in your voice. This is not a time to scold, but an opportunity to offer guidance, "It is not safe to throw a fork, but you may throw a ball."

In similar situations with young children who have more experience at the table, you may see them put their flatware in their glass. They notice it makes an interesting noise. They continue to do this. This is an important opportunity to set your expectation for appropriate behavior at the table. "Oh, I hear that interesting sound. Please put your fork to the left of your plate." Why do we do this? Some say, "Let children be children. Let them play." Yes, children should play. However, they look to us to help them understand the social norms and if we abandon them in this moment, by allowing them to play with their water and their dishes, we miss an opportunity for them to become more independent in their self-control and in their social interactions. If we don't show them now when they are so receptive to learning the customs of our culture, then when do we show them? It is best fro them to learn when the risk is low, at home in a moment of calm. This same behavior in a restaurant or at a family gathering can be more difficult to manage. When you set your expectations daily, at home, in a familiar space, your child has the confidence and experience to be independent in appropriate social interactions, outside of your home.

As for water play, and interesting sounds, these are great activities for playtime. Outside in the yard, a child can explore with water; pouring, splashing, and swirling. Or consider bath time with containers to transfer water. When children have open-ended playtime, they make important discoveries.

— Part II —
Family Meals

"The preparation of good food is merely another expression of art, one of the joys of civilized living…"

— Dione Lucas

*"If you really want to make a friend, go to someone's house and eat with him...
the people who give you their food give you their heart."*

— *Cesar Chavez*

When my three children were babies, I would take them to the farmers market or grocery store and talk about what we would be making and the ingredients we needed. I invited them to help me choose the produce, talking about what makes a good choice for each item. As they became more capable in the kitchen, I asked them to get a saucepan, or frying pan from the cupboard. I was teaching them the names of the tools we use. They could feel the difference in the weight of each pan and hear the sounds as they carefully tried to remove them from the shelves. All of these sensorial experiences helping to build their knowledge of their world. They have always helped me to cook and prepare food. Now, they often ask to prepare a particular dish themselves to contribute to the meal or they ask if I will teach them to make their favorites. While we cook side-by-side they tell stories of their day or discuss our plans for the weekend.

Keeping open communication feels natural in the kitchen. We can even work side-by-side without speaking. We are working in partnership toward a common goal—dinner. We each contribute to the same meal—taking care of one another and the family—and being there, we are available to each other.

There are so many benefits to family meals. Research[2] shows that families that have three or more meals together each week have children with:

- Better academic performance
- Higher self-esteem
- Greater sense of resilience
- Lower risk of teen pregnancy

- Lower risk of substance abuse
- Lower risk of depression
- Lower rates of obesity
- Lower likelihood of developing eating disorders

As a parent, I look at this list and I think we cannot afford to NOT have regular family meals. It is essential that we make time to sit together, have conversation, and enjoy food.

Families can find a time, daily, when the whole family comes together for a meal and even make space for your infant. This becomes more difficult as children get older and have their own schedules with sports practices, clubs, and friends. However, if you start this family ritual from your first meals together, your child will internalize the importance and make time and adjustments to their schedule in order to participate in family meals.

As with everything in life, meals have a beginning, middle, and an end. Parents can model and include children in as much of the process as possible. This will change depending on their ages, experience, and coordination. Infants will be observers to all of the parts while young children and older children should be involved in some aspect of each part of the meal.

With a Montessori lens, we would see this type of participation as part of daily life and an essential experience in the life of the family. However, often in our culture, helping with meals falls in the category of chores. In her 2016 TED talk, Julie Lythcott-Haims explains that the longest longitudinal study of humans ever conducted, The Harvard Grant Study, "found that professional success in life comes from doing chores and the earlier you start, the better." She also explains that "self-efficacy is built when one sees that one's own actions lead to outcomes." Children who grow up with regular responsibilities within their family learn to care for themselves and others and have the internal belief that they are capable.[3]

Allow your child to grow in independence and participation as he gains more skills. Often, as parents, it is easy to get in the habit of doing things *for* your child and overlook how he grows more and more capable. Depending on your child's temperament, he may be happy to let you do for him, or he may protest. If your child allows you to do for him, it may be more difficult for you to recognize when he is ready for more responsibility.

As a family you will work out who is responsible for which roles. There may be times when parents prepare the meals and children set and clear the table, or vice versa. A family meal is a group effort and everyone in the family should be a part of the experience. Everyone's presence and everyone's participation matters.

This section is devoted to describing each element of the family meal and how each member of the family can play an active role. The elements of the family meal are; meal planning, a trip to the market, food preparation, setting the table, expressions of gratitude, conversation, grace and courtesy, and the clean up.

Meal Planning

"A recipe is a story that ends with a good meal."

-Pat Conroy

Meal Planning can involve almost any age child. Infants who are eating solid food can start to contribute to meal planning. Even the youngest child can help make choices when choosing between squash or carrots and berries or pears. Show your child two options, name them, and see which she chooses.

Children as young as two or three can start to help plan meals. Ask them which vegetable they would like with dinner, or to name a type of bread that could be served. Once you have determined the meal, talk through the ingredients and ask them to look in the pantry for the ingredients. They can help contribute to a list of groceries. Reading children can help find recipes and writing children can write grocery lists.

A Trip to the Market

"The odds of going to the store for a loaf of bread and coming out
with only a loaf of bread are three billion to one."

— Erma Bombeck

I love the market. I always have. Trips to the market are some of my favorite memories with my young children and continue to be memorable with my now teenagers. So often I see children in carts with a personal screen in their hands. They are watching a program or playing with a cartoon game. They are missing out on the wonders all around. Instead of giving your child a screen at the market, consider the market as a developmental wonderland! The opportunities for education at the market are endless. Once you see the market through this lens, you will need to plan more time for your trips to the market.

A trip to the market is an important experience for all children in your family, from infancy through the teen years. When you go to the store with younger children, it is helpful to verbalize expectations before you enter. When I would go to the market with an infant, 1year old, and three year old, I would make sure to say to all three, "we are going into the market, we have some items we need for dinner tonight. We will gather those items, I need your help. We will then pay for the items and put them in our car." This may seem like I explained a lot, but children often need to know the plan in order to be helpful in executing that plan. Once you have let them know, they can follow the step-by-step routine with you and in coordination with your efforts.

In order to help you set reasonable expectations for your age child, I have outlined the many ways a child experiences and benefits from a trip to the market. The following charts can help you maximize your experience.

	At The Market — Infants
Language development	Talk with your child about all of the produce and foods that you see. Have a conversation about what you are preparing for meals that week.
Social Development	Other people at the market will naturally smile at you and your baby. This is an opportunity for you to show your baby how to say hello. This may also be a way to show your baby how to set limits. Many people reach out to touch babies without permission. It is okay for you to say to your baby, "I think this woman wants to say hello, can you wave? Hello" make the waving motion. Even if your baby can not make the waving motion yet, you are helping to set a boundary for your child that saying hello does not require touching.
Sensorial Exploration	When choosing produce, you can show your child different textures. Invite her to touch the mango and ugly fruit. Name each fruit as your child touches it.

Conversation at the Market

For children who are talking, play the question game. It can help to reiterate the lessons from the garden and farm. Ask your child a series of questions on the same topic that require more than a "yes" or "no" response.

Example:		
	Parent:	"What did you eat for breakfast?"
	Child:	"Eggs, toast, and strawberries."
	Parent:	"Where did the eggs come from?"
	Child:	"From the refrigerator."
	Parent:	"How did they get in the refrigerator?"
	Child:	"I put them there."
	Parent:	"Where did you get the eggs?"
	Child:	"From the store."
	Parent:	"Where did the store get the eggs?"
	Child:	"From the chickens."
	Parent:	"Where are the chickens?"
	Child:	"On the farm."

At The Market — Young Walking Children

Language Development	Your child is learning that everything has a name. He may want to point at different food and you can say the name. He is learning what words and objects go together so you can start to help him classify the different foods. Tell him; "This is the vegetable section. We are going to choose some vegetables for our salad tonight." Then name them as you choose them.
Social Development	Your child will meet many new people at the market and may even see some familiar faces. This is a great opportunity to model introducing yourself, saying hello to friends, or even a short conversation with the cashier, "Hello. How are you today? Thank you, Have a great day." Your child is learning from you all these important social expectations.
Sensorial Exploration	Each item he touches gives him new information to understand and classify. Take the time to name and give him experience holding different foods. He will feel the different textures and weights. In the produce section, allow him to taste the samples of fruits and veggies that are offered. Many stores have an area where a child can choose a piece of fruit to snack on during their visit.
Movement	He will need to move and may not want to always sit in the cart while you push him. It is important to honor this need for movement and accommodate when possible. If he is trying to get out of the cart, say, "I need your help to choose some cereal. Can you choose this box of corn flakes or this box of granola?" The aisles of the store can be overwhelming so try to minimize the choices by narrowing it down to two. This is also a time your child is looking to exert maximum effort. He may want to challenge himself by carrying the largest box of cereal or the heaviest bag of potatoes. When possible, let him do this, It can be a very satisfying experience for him.
Independence	In order to employ his help and engagement in the trip to the market, you can ask him to hold a bag while you choose produce. Place the bag next to him in the cart or stroller and hand him the fruit saying, "one orange, two oranges…" he can then place each one in the bag. He can also be responsible to carry the reusable bags from home.

	At The Market — Children Who Can Write And Read
Language Development	Now that your child can write and read, it is a great time to make him in charge of the grocery list. Ask him to read the next item on the list, and show him to put a check after you have gathered each item.
Social Development	Since your child has been watching you model social interaction, he may wish to engage in his own conversation with people he meets at the market. This is a time that parents get nervous about what their child might say. This is because young children say what is on their mind and often do not understand what conversation fits the context of casual grocery store conversation. If this happens, acknowledge what your child said and then say, "I understand that you made that observation. That is something you can think and maybe not share out loud. Sometimes you can have a thought and you don't have to say it in the moment."
Sensorial Exploration	At this stage it is great to show your child how to choose ripe produce. Discuss the texture density and smell of produce that is ready for consumption. This will help them refine their senses and build their understanding of how fruits and veggies grow.
Mathematical Exploration	Use this time to take advantage of your child's natural tendency to count, notice pattern, and calculate. Invite your child to gather fruits and vegetables, asking for specific numbers. Introduce the scale and how to read the weight.
Movement	Many markets offer small shopping carts or hand held baskets. Your child can carry or push their own basket to fill with the items on the list.
Independence	Keeping track of the list, choosing from the shelves, and carrying their own basket are all important moments for independence. You can also empower your child by asking her to choose a loaf of bread to go with a pasta dinner, a dessert to make, or even a beverage to have with meals. Giving choice and the freedom to make decisions helps build her self-confidence as well as awareness of others' preferences.

At The Market — Children Six To Twelve Years Old	
Language development	Children become very interested in the origins of words and the details and specifics of where things come from. Offer your child a book with latin names of fruits and veggies and ask them to only choose fruits of veggies from particular countries. This helps them to learn from where produce comes.
Social Development	Your child is now completely capable of carrying on a conversation with those he meets at the market. Encourage him to do all the verbal exchange with the cashier, ordering something from the deli or bakery, and even casual conversation with anyone else who may helping to bag or carry your groceries.
Mathematical Exploration	Ask him to estimate the weight of an item before using the scale and ask him to calculate the price after identifying the weight.
Independence	Now aware of ingredients and amounts, allow your child to measure and weigh items in bulk. He can also take part in calculating costs, estimate total purchase amount, and complete transactions at the register. He can learn to watch as the amounts add up to catch if a price does not match what a shelf was labeled.

	At The Market — Middle And High School
Independence	By now your child is capable of meal planning, recipe selection, and grocery list making. She can also do independent trips to the store and return home to help prepare a meal. Your child's previous experiences with you at the market to learn to communicate, find what he needs, measure, and estimate were all preparation for this moment when she can step away from the family, gather the items the family needs, and return with her contribution to the family meal. I often ask one of my teenagers to run back to the store for an item I forgot.

Teenagers: Social Skill Building at the Market

During a recent visit to the market, my teenager asked why I chose to go to that particular store, when there was a different one closer to our house. I explained that I liked the layout of the store as well as the friendliness of the people who worked at this market better. While the cashier scanned all of our groceries, I chatted with him about the recipes we would be making. The cashier was friendly and was asking questions and initiated the conversation. On our way out, my son asked, "Mom, was that O.K. for the cashier to ask you all those questions, or was that weird?" This was a great question. I am so glad he asked. I was happy to explain that this was socially appropriate and I got to learn a little about the cashier and he got to learn about our choice in groceries. We were two people connecting in this big city; not for the purpose of forming a friendship, but for the purpose of being connected to other people through story and conversation. It was not weird at all. For my teen, he is still trying to figure out what information do you share with strangers, when is it ok to engage in conversation with strangers, and that most people in this world are not out to harm you. Interaction is good. Conversation is good. It can connect us and it builds community.

Food Preparation

"A good cook is like a sorceress who dispenses happiness."

— Elsa Schiaparelli

The preparation of a family meal can be done by one person or by any combination of members of the family. Infants may want to watch the preparation or play nearby while you work. Once a child is aware of food preparation they often want to be a part of the process. A Learning Tower or Kitchen Helper can aid standing children with this. Even if they are only going to watch with the aid of the above-mentioned safety-tested devices, they can be brought to counter height safely to see the process. You can start including your child in the process with washing fruits and vegetables in a colander at the sink. As you and your child are ready, introduce more complex tasks that help contribute to the meal.

Your child can use simple snack-preparation skills to help with meal preparation. For example, if he has recently learned to slice, incorporate a fruit salad in the menu. If he has learned to spread, include a recipe with butter on bread or cream cheese on celery. When you include recipes where a young child can contribute, it helps him feel connected to his family and to understand that he is capable and welcome. As he grows he will start to initiate preparing food for the family. There are two types of food preparation; preparing food with your child and independent food preparation.

"This is my invariable advice to people:
Learn how to cook- try new recipes,
learn from your mistakes,
be fearless, and above all have fun!"

— Julia Child

Preparing Food *With* Children

"Cooking is at once child's play and adult joy. And cooking done with care is an act of love."

-Craig Claiborne

Your child wants to be a part of family life. From the time he begins eating solid food, he becomes interested in the preparation of food. He wants to see how food is made, where the sounds and smells are coming from, and he will probably ask you to hold him and show him things in the kitchen while you are making dinner. This can be difficult.

Once he is supporting himself in a standing position you can offer a stool that is designed to safely allow children to stand at counter height. Although his skills and coordination may be limited, your child has a strong urge to be part of the process of preparing food and providing for others. He gains a great sense of pride by participating in the preparation of food. This is one reason Montessori schools have a focus on food preparation.

By inviting your child to be a part of this process you help to open them up to some important learning experiences:

• Learn what goes into their food

• Gain an understanding of recipes and ingredients

• Learn from where their food comes

• Become more willing to try new tastes, textures, and food combinations

• Experience providing and caring for others

• Feel connection to the activities of the family

• Care for their own needs, allowing them to learn new skills and contribute in a larger way

• Understand their own body signals around food including feelings of hunger

• Practice of fine motor skills

• Building concentration

• Experience successful cycle of activity — beginning, middle, and end

• Build their vocabulary

• Refine their senses so as to better discriminate small differences leading to greater appreciation of taste, smell, and texture

Each child has their own personality and it is important to honor that in the kitchen. Some are adventurous, some chatty, others quiet, and others more cautious. There is room for everyone. My rule is to create opportunity for my children to contribute as they are curious and interested. Each child gets a chance to work alongside me, without their siblings and at other times, with their siblings.

Meal preparations that include everyone in the family are wonderful. It is important to have both one-on-one experiences as well as group experiences.

Helping vs. Hovering

Keeping your child safe is of-course most important. However, as parents, it may be difficult to know when we are keeping them safe and when we are getting in their way. It can help to understand when you are hovering and when you are helping.

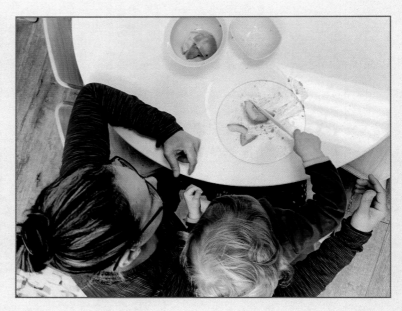

Hovering comes from the adult's worry about the child completing a task in a certain way or in a certain time frame, or needing to protect or save their child from either injury or failure. Hovering stems from a belief that a child is not capable. As parents, we hover when we think we have to do something for the child.

Three signs you might be hovering:

1. When you watch your child doing a task and you think: "that's cute but she needs to really do it better."

2. When your child finishes a task, looks to you, and your first response is to correct her work (wiping the table better or refolding the napkins).

3. When your child is, for example, cutting a banana and you step in *before* watching to see if she can do it safely on her own (tip: breathe and count to five; does she still need your help?).

Helping comes from a place of trust and allows a parent to take an observer's role. When we step back and make ourselves available for help, we leave it to the child to determine when he needs assistance. We ask open-ended check-in questions like, "How's it going?" that allow him to ask for help (in words, expressions, or actions). *Helping* supports the development of self-confidence and resilience. When we allow a child to struggle and push through without our hovering, the child develops problem-solving skills, confidence, and concentration.

Independent Food Preparation

"No one who cooks, cooks alone. Even at her most solitary, a cook in the kitchen is surrounded by generations of cooks past, the advice and menus of cooks present, the wisdom of cookbook writers."

— Laurie Colwin

Once you have shown your child to use a food preparation tool properly and you have seen her demonstrate that she can repeat the use safely, she is ready for independent food preparation. Some children start around twelve months old. You might start with something that is simple like peeling tangerines and then later, once you are comfortable, move to slicing bananas or pickles. Once a child understands the process and the importance of using tools properly, she will be able to make scrambled eggs and then move on to more complicated baking recipes. *Always be present in the kitchen when your child is using tools and hot surfaces.* Remember not to hover.

Parenting is a constant balance of supporting your child's development and letting her learn on her own, sometimes through failure. It is difficult to know when to step in and when to step back. Observation is the key to knowing the difference. It is important to acknowledge that you won't always get it right. When you step back to observe you can make a clear decision to step in if your child is using a tool in an unsafe way or needs a re-presentation in order to use the tool properly. Remember independent work does not mean unsupervised.

It is helpful to remain nearby and observant should he need guidance. Hovering sends the message that you are not confident in his abilities. It also can make you more nervous as you may be more prone to step in and take over if you watch each step. Be confident that he can handle the materials you have shown him to use. He will feel your confidence in him and his own self-confidence will grow. Consider occupying yourself with a mundane nearby task that allows you to observe while you work, intervene or assist if called for, and does not give your child an impression of you being in their work space.

Sometimes your child may doubt his ability to be independent. Here are some ways to work through his doubt and support his independence:

• *Use Words of Encouragement* "You have mixed batter many times before. Maybe you need to try again to get all the ingredients mixed."

• *Work Collaboratively* "Lets slice the strawberries together, I'll slice this one, which one will you slice?"

• *Ask a Question* "I see the batter is stuck in the whisk. Do we have another tool that might be better for mixing this batter?"

A Note on Mistakes

It is important for your child to experience both successes and failures. It is through both that she will learn control of movement, perseverance, self-control, and reliance. She will challenge herself through learning the limits of her capabilities. She may find that success is defined by the taste of the food and not its visual presentation. Let that be her decision and discovery. She will grow through the process of her work and come to have her own opinions about the product.

Acknowledge your child's efforts. If you sit together to enjoy the food she prepares, mention the different flavors, or name some of the ingredients she used in the process. Encourage her with comments like, "I can smell the cinnamon you used in these muffins," or "Thank you for preparing food for us to share." Avoid static statements like, "You are such a good girl." Make comments about your child's effort and your own gratitude rather than about your child's character.

Sample Menu for Food Preparation With Your Child

Once your child has begun preparing food with you and engaged in some independent food preparation, consider making a weekly schedule for who will prepare food and what they will make. This is the perfect way to then introduce your child to making a grocery list! Once they are reading, they can look up the recipes you have chosen and make a list of the items you need at the market. Below is a sample weekly plan for including your child(ren) in food preparation.

Day	What	Who	Meal
Monday	Bake Muffins	Together	For Tuesday breakfast
Tuesday	Slice fruit	Independently, each child has a fruit to prepare	For Tuesday dinner
Wednesday	Roast sweet potatoes	Together, with one child	For Wednesday dinner
Thursday	Bake a casserole	Together	For Thursday dinner
Friday	Spread nut butter on crackers	Independently, each child can prepare a portion	For Friday snack
Saturday	Bake bread	Together, with one child	Saturday Dinner
Sunday	Shop	Together	For next week's meals

Connect Your Child to Their Food Source

"It's difficult to think anything but pleasant thoughts while eating a homegrown tomato."

— Lewis Grizzard

For young children, it is important that they are connected to the source of their food. Knowing where our food comes from helps us to understand how the world works. Young children only know what is in their environment, and when their home includes stories of how things are made and books about gardening, and plants to water and grow, they learn that our actions are connected to other living beings. When food shows up on the table already prepared and ready to eat, they do not have a natural connection to the origins of their food.

When you shop at the market with your child, choose whole foods so they can see how those foods are prepared to be part of a recipe.

Visiting a farm or growing food at your house shows your child the origins of their food. Even a small pot of herbs outside your door helps connect your child to the natural process of growing food. After nurturing, watering, and pruning a plant, they can pick the fruit, slice it, and add it to a recipe.

Connecting to food sources is also helpful for eggs and milk. It is great for a child to learn that chickens lay eggs, how they roost, and how to gather the eggs. This takes the mystery out of meals and gives children concrete, accurate information about the world.

Setting the Table

"Pull up a chair. Take a taste. Come join us. Life is so endlessly delicious."

— Ruth Reichl

Starting from the first meal, introduce the place setting. Using an outlined placemat as the template, set a plate, fork, spoon, and glass (pictured on page 20). Your child can see that everything has a place. Continue to use this placemat layout at every meal and snacks and once your child is walking, he will be able to set his own place. Once he internalizes the layout of a place setting (at about two-and-a-half years old), you no longer need the template on the placemat and your child can independently set the table if he can reach where the dishes are stored.

Setting the table can be a job for any walking child. Giving children direct access to their dishes and flatware helps him to work independently and at his own pace. It can be helpful to have a set of children's dishes in a low cabinet to support children's independence around meals and eating. By using breakable dishes from the start and showing how to hold one item at a time, he will then work to walk back and forth, adding to the table carefully, with all the items needed for your family meal.

Show your child to carry one item at a time or to use a basket to gather the needed pieces before taking them all to the table. Moving back and forth to the table incorporates movement with the intellectual task of remembering the items he needs. This is an integrative learning experience for him. Remember, moving is learning! Parents often want to hurry this process for efficiency's sake, but it is important for a young child to experience repetition over efficiency. This is the same process for clearing the table.

When you start early on, including your child in the steps of setting the table, around three years old, they start to spontaneously set the table when they see it's meal time. This may not be at every meal and it may not even always be at meal time. However, they do start to become aware of the need and their connection to their family through this process. It is important to have the dishes accessible to your child for this reason. Some families have a separate cabinet or buffet to hold the dishes, where other families designate an existing cabinet in the kitchen.

However you store the dishes, keep in mind that the items should be kept in a consistent place with a consistent order. If this area becomes cluttered or disorganized, a child is less able to be independent with setting the table.

Children six and older are able to consistently gather items from different places. If your children are all moving into this stage of development or beyond, you can keep the dishes separate; plates in one cabinet, flatware in a drawer, glasses in another cabinet, etc. If you have one child in the older stage and still younger children, I recommend keeping the single organized cabinet for all the children to access.

Choosing Dishes, Furniture, and Tools

Whether it is your child's first meal or his five-hundredth, the dishes and furniture you choose will be a factor in his experience and success in self-feeding. It is important to consider the size, weight, material, and durability of the items you choose. All of these items should be sized for your child. The actual size depends on the age of your child. Flatware that is sized for a one-year-old is different than flatware designed for a four-year-old.

Children are most successfully independent when their environment is consistent and the routine is predictable. Both of these depend on the preparation of the environment and the choices you make in the furniture and dishes you offer.

Low Table and Chairs

The first meal is given at the weaning table and chair that is low and sturdy so that your child's feet reach the floor and he feels steady (see page 19 for more details). The chair should have arms, a straight back, and a cushion or non-skid layer to keep him from slipping out of the chair. Anti-slip rug pads make a good temporary non-skid surface.

The weaning table and chair is used until he is crawling and pulling-up and ready for a chair he can get in and out of on his own. The second chair should be a steady low chair with an 8" seat height with no arms. This allows him to pull the chair out and sit comfortably at the table. This is typically introduced around twelve months. This chair can be used at the weaning table, or you can introduce a little taller and lighter weight table at this time.

Once your child is walking with ease and steady on his feet—around two-years old—he can use a typical child's table and chair set. These are the most common table and chairs sold for young children. Many companies such as Guidecraft, Pottery Barn Kids, and Ikea sell tables and chairs this height. You could also make your own child-sized table from scratch or by cutting down the legs on a taller table. Refer to the chart on page 54 for measurements. Many side tables and coffee tables can be altered in this way.

High Chairs

At the family table, use a high chair with straps to keep your baby secure. Pull this chair to the table without a tray so that everyone shares the same eating surface. Sharing the table surface creates an atmosphere of inclusion, shared experience, connection, and conversation.   AN infant will need the straps in a chair for safety, however, once your child is able to get in and out of the chair on his own, the straps may no longer be needed. See page 55 for more details about a high chair.

Dishes, Utensils, and Tools

In order for your young child to be successful in self-feeding and food preparation, he needs access to dishes, tools, and utensils that are real and properly sized. This means that it should fit in his hand, not be too heavy, and work well for the task for which it is intended. So often, children are given items that are plastic, flimsy, or made as toys. These cause frustration when children try to use them as a real tool for a real purpose.

Ceramic, porcelain, and glass dishes create a beautiful presentation, teach care of breakable objects, and convey a respect for the young child's capabilities. Even very young children can learn to use breakable dishes and handle them properly. When the dishes are sized proportionately to the child's abilities, a ceramic plate is easy for a child to use.

Children want to participate in family life like all other family members. They recognize when the items they are given are different from others. Respect your child's ability to be careful; offer him real dishes, not plastic ones. He will appreciate, value, and internalize the inclusive nature of your choice. This internalized value adds to his developing self-confidence and self-respect. Show him how to carry these items, one at a time. Show him, and then give him a turn. Take turns like this until he shows he understands the care needed. If you show him in a way that is slowed down, and a bit exaggerated (but not overly dramatic) in careful walking, he will watch and repeat.

Choose flatware that is metal and sturdy. Do not use utensils that are coated with rubber or silicone. Metal forks with real tines are easiest for spearing food and will improve the chances of success for self-feeding. Likewise with a metal spoon; it is the best tool for scooping and self-feeding. Your child may be frustrated and might even give-up on self-feeding if his utensils are too thick, not sharp enough, or difficult to use.

The tools that your child uses to prepare food are a key part of your child's success. Tools have a specific intended purpose. Show your child the right tool to use for each task. This helps to keep your child safe and gives clear guidelines. If your child misuses a tool, just remove the tool and say, "That is not how it is to be used. We will put it away for another day." This helps your child understand the importance of using tools properly in order to stay safe. It is important to set reasonable limits from the beginning. Even children who are not yet speaking are capable of understanding limits. Clear and consistent limits help a child feel safe and understand expectations. A child learns to keep herself safe and on-task.

As she uses real tools alongside you she develops concentration. Repetition with real tools and consistent guidelines creates a safe environment to use knives, peelers, ceramic dishes, and glasses. When children understand the expectations of their environment, they are able to make informed choices. A child who misuses a tool is reassured when the parent enforces the rule and removes the tool once it is misused. It is this routine (child tests, adult reenforces) that creates a safe work environment in the kitchen. Children can be trusted with tools when they work alongside an adult who themselves can be trusted to consistently enforce the rules.

Dishes and Furniture Sizing by Age

Item	Age	Size
Flatware	6 to 36 months	3"-4" long (7-10 cm)
	3 to 6 years	5"-7" long (13-18 cm)
Tools	12 months to six years	5"-7" long (13-18 cm)
Serving Utensils	12 months to six years	5"-7" long (13-18 cm)
Plate	6 to 12 months	5"-6" across (13-15 cm)
	12 months to six years	6"-7" across (15-18 cm)
Glass	6 to 12 months	2-3 oz (60-90 ml)
	12 to 30 months	5-7 oz (150-210 ml)
	30 months to six years	10 oz (300 ml)
Table	6 to 12 months	12" tall (30 cm)
	12 to 30 months	14"-16" tall (35-40 cm)
	3 to 5 years	20"-24" tall (50-60 cm)
	6 to 9 years	27"-30" tall (68-76 cm)
Chair	6 to 12 months	5" seat (13 cm)
	12 to 30 months	7"-9" seat (18-23 cm)
	3 to 5 years	12"-15" seat (30-38 cm)
	6 to 9 years	14"-19" seat (35-49 cm)

High Chair for Independence

A high chair is used at the family table and includes straps to keep your baby secure. Pull this chair to the table without a tray so that you and your child share the same eating surface. We purchased an adjustable chair for each of our children so that the seat height and foot rest could be moved as they grew. They continued to use their chairs into their elementary years. Being comfortable, made of wood, easy to clean, and convertible made them a great long term investment. We chose the Tripp Trapp® chair from Stokke® in a different color for each child. When we moved to our new house, I planned to sell the three chairs as they were still in good condition and another family would get good use out of them. Our children were all able to sit at the family table in adult size chairs at that point. When I loaded them into the car one morning to deliver them to a neighborhood buyer, my children were crushed. They wanted to keep their chairs. This is where they sat, all their lives. Where we had so many conversations and shared so many meals. They were not ready to let them go. It was that moment that reinforced how important our family meals are. We started  when they were infants and we have no plans to stop. We decided to keep the chairs and maybe someday they can each have them at their family tables with their own children.

Gratitude

In the culture in which we are raising our children, it is common to pause before eating a meal to say a prayer, have a moment of silence, or share words or thoughts of gratitude. My husband and I decided that we would take time before meals to have a moment of gratitude. We hold hands and each person has a chance to name something for which they are thankful. We started this when we had one little boy sitting at the table. Now with three children, two of whom are teenagers, we continue to do this at each family meal. When we have guests, we include them; they, too have the opportunity to share a thought of gratitude or words of thanks. Sometimes I think back to those moments when our eldest was a year old and he held our hands and listened as we named our gratitude. He only had a few single words at that time and he waited quietly, as we modeled our values—what he would one day be able and interested to do. Today, our eldest is often the first to name for what he is grateful. Each of our children understands that it is an important part of our meal.

Pausing to be grateful has given me insight into what my children hold dear and where their thoughts are that day. Sometimes they are grateful for the food in front of them and other days they name every member of their family. If they got help from a friend they may say, "I am grateful for good friends." If they had an argument with their brother they may even say, "I am thankful I don't have to sit next to my brother tonight." Each time they pause and think about what they have or what could be different, we grow as a family and in our understanding of one another.

It is not joy that makes us grateful, it is gratitude that makes us joyful.

— David Steindl-Rast

Conversation

"You can't just eat good food. You've got to talk about it too. And you've got to talk about it to somebody who understands that kind of food."

— Kurt Vonnegut

Sometimes it can be difficult to make conversation. Young children are learning to make conversation. Participation and contributions can be variable. Each stage of your child's development brings about new skills, growing abilities, and even some surprises in conversation.

When your baby is small and you hold him in your arms as you eat, or as he is in a bassinet next to the table, you are including him in the family meal. You are telling him that he is part of the family and there is a place at the table for him. From this early age you are also laying a psychological foundation for him that your family values and desires his presence.

Conversation with a pre-verbal baby is challenging because it takes great intention and mindfulness on your part to keep the conversation going. It is easy to start with a question, a smile of acknowledgement, and then slip right back into your quiet thoughts. It is okay to take pauses in conversation. Enjoying the quiet together is also time well-spent. When you ask questions, pause for baby to kick, smile, coo, or give some other response. Then continue with another question or even a story. I often found myself telling my children about a dream I had the night before or something I saw during a visit to the store. All of it is interesting to them because it is coming from you. Your children love to hear your voice and they are learning the rhythm and intonation of your language from your conversation. They are studying the pauses and cadence of your words. Conversation is free and makes a significant difference in children's developing communication, language skills, vocabulary and social engagement.

Between one and two-years-old, your child can contribute to conversation with words. It can feel easier on parents and is often delightful! You will hear words and phrases that make you smile, prompt new questions, or even make you laugh. Conversational exchange has begun. One difficulty that can occur in conversation with a young child is that it also comes with strong emotion. Since they often don't have quite enough words to communicate their feelings, we are often met with the word "no," throwing objects, or hand pounding to emphasize their discontentment.

Sometimes the words of a young child can be difficult to understand, which can cause greater frustration. If you find you are not sure what your child is saying, ask, "Can you show me?" If needed, allow him to get up from his seat so that he can point to or touch what he is talking about. Young children think concretely; often, the thing or person they are talking about is in the room. Once he has shown you, say clearly the name of what he has shown you and then ask him to return to the table and continue your meal.

A three- to five-year-old child has stories to tell, and their perspective can be enlightening. Usually just a well-timed question or inquisitive look can spur a memory or a description that takes them down their own stream of consciousness path. As they learn to share stories, they can have difficulty pausing to let others talk, or even to take a bite. I always felt our longest meals were during the years that our children were between the ages of three and six, each child having their own pace and contribution to the conversation.

Between the ages of six and twelve, a child is building, testing, and sharing a wealth of knowledge. He is excited about learning and wants to share the details of research he is doing at school, a book he got at the library, or the exciting story his friend shared. Through family meals, my children have talked about physics and the earth's rotation, theories of time (and questions about whether it really exists), and the names and stories of Greek, Roman, and Norse gods and goddesses. I've learned so much from and about my children from these conversations.

This is also a time when family dinners can become harder to coordinate with differing schedules, especially if there are sports or extracurricular activities. A child eats many different foods at this age and, at times, you may find it easier to grab something on the go.

Before deciding on the drive-thru or take out, I find it helpful to review this short list of questions:

1. Does this really take less time than boiling pasta and throwing together a salad?

2. What am I modeling by eating in the car?

3. Of all the days this week, how many will I resort to going picking up take-out?

4. Is this a *treat* or a regular occurrence (habit or pattern)?

Once your child is in her early teens, the strong emotions are back. What you may have thought was an innocent question has resulted in the reaction of storming off to her room. There maybe times when this is unavoidable. Dealing with real emotions—highs and lows—in a conscious way is part of her journey to adulthood. When she does this at home, this is a safe place. (A meal at home helps to keep emotional outbursts private and not on display.) Sharing a meal at home brings to light all the feelings of comfort that you have had since she was an infant. She feels those and wants to be there. She feels the connection.

Your young teen may sometimes not feel much like contributing to conversation. (Sometimes you may not feel like having conversation either!) Being there together is important to the continued connection of the family. You may sometimes hear more sarcastic responses than authentic contribution to the conversation. She is trying to find a way that her unique voice can be heard (stand out) in the family. Try not to react emotionally to the sarcasm; respond with kindness and honesty. When your child hears your consistent and kind attitude towards her, she will, in time, change her tune back to a more productive form of conversation.

In his later teens, his independence has grown so much. He makes his own plans and may now even get around town independently. It is important that he has freedom, yet it is also important that he stay connected to you through family meals. It might have been the case that when he was younger, dinner was the main family meal many times a week. In the teen years, dinner might not be the easiest; maybe it will be getting up earlier and making breakfast together some days. Ask him in the beginning of the week which days he will be home for dinner (or other family meals) and how he can contribute. Will he want to cook or pick up the ingredients at the store on his way home? Continuing to contribute to family life helps him to stay connected and have a purposeful role in the family, where you are counting on him. Having responsibility to be with the family helps him balance his personal interests with those of his community.

When your teenager has some meals away from home or with friends, it is an important step in his establishing his own patterns. During adolescence, pushing back on family rules and pre-existing patterns is normal. Those actions are an important part of growing up and establishing an adult identity.

I cannot stress enough the importance of the conversations that happen around family meals. Each conversation gives me insight into what our children are thinking, and how they are processing their experiences while growing up.

At Studio June, all of our classes for children one year and older have a meal component. We offer this for a couple reasons. First, the children learn to independently set the table in an environment that is prepared just for them. Secondly, parents learn how to let their child serve themselves and feed themselves as the instructor leads the meal. Additionally, the children have the opportunity to sit across from their friends and talk about their meal, their activity of the day, or just about anything else that comes to mind. We provide an opportunity for spontaneous conversation among peers.

Grace and Courtesy

"Manners are a sensitive awareness of the feelings of others. If you have that awareness, you have good manners, no matter what fork you use."

— Emily Post

In Montessori practice, grace and courtesy are opportunities to share customs, traditions, and social expectations with our children through modeling and practice. We cannot make a child say "please" and "thank you", however, we can always model the desired behavior and then give children chances to practice as well as to use the words in real situations. Mealtime provides many opportunities to practice grace and courtesy.

Mealtime Grace and Courtesy

- Saying "thank you"

- Saying grace or giving gratitude

- Taking food and then passing it along

- Asking for food

- Waiting patiently

- Taking a fair helping of food

- Asking to be excused from the table

- Complimenting the chef

- Interrupting a conversation

- Clearing someone's dishes

- Serving someone else

- Introducing the ingredients in a recipe

- Receiving a compliment

- Waiting to start eating until everyone has been served

In our home, we introduced grace and courtesy as soon as our children were born as often as a fitting occasion arose, by being conscious about the language we used with our infants as well as with each other. Once they were talking we started to hear our words repeated back to us. Young children repeat the language they hear around them, often in the appropriate situation. Between the ages of four and twelve, our children used their knowledge freely and we heard many natural expressions of their gratitude. Once our children started to become teenagers, I sensed a loss in the use of niceties from them. I don't think this was conscious on their part, but I was

conscious of it. I saw the change as a call for us to be more intentional again in our own presentation and modeling of grace and courtesy. The conscious effort on our part has allowed us to have conversations with our children about cultural norms, expectations, and the choices we make in these situations. I believe this makes them more confident and aware in their community.

In Montessori schools, grace and courtesy lessons are given in two ways: directly and indirectly. Direct lessons happen in prepared and thought-out gatherings in which a teacher invites the children to watch how to do a particular activity or task such as greeting someone or offering tea to someone. Then the teacher acts out this scenario with the children. When she is done, the children are invited to practice the scenario. Indirect lessons are the daily interactions that happen naturally within the class. When the teacher passes and says, "pardon me" or when she welcomes them in the morning and shakes each child's hand saying, "good morning." These indirect lessons are the most natural way to include grace and courtesy in your home environment.

When you model the use of manners and culturally appropriate interactions, you show your children your expectations of language and behavior in social situations. You have many opportunities in the day to demonstrate what you expect to see in your child. When you model this at home consistently, you will see your child spontaneously and correctly repeat the same niceties in public.

Clean Up

"One cannot think well, love well, sleep well, if one has not dined well."

— Virginia Woolf

Every family handles the after-meal clean up differently. For a young child who can walk, that may mean he takes his plate to the sink or dishwasher. For an older child, he may also help to clear serving dishes. Older children can find containers in which to store leftovers, and almost every age child can wipe the table with a wet sponge or cloth. Even an infant in a high chair can wipe an area of the table with a small sponge.

The clean up is not to be overlooked. It is essential that children learn the end of each activity. Learning to complete a cycle is essential in their understanding of accomplishment and the feeling of success. The beginning, the middle, and the end are all important. The beginning is the effort of making a choice, the middle is acting on the choice, and the end is working until completion, moving through struggles to find closure. Once we are able to *complete* one activity, we are then free to make a new choice. It is this flow that keeps us moving forward in life with new knowledge and understanding of ourselves and others.

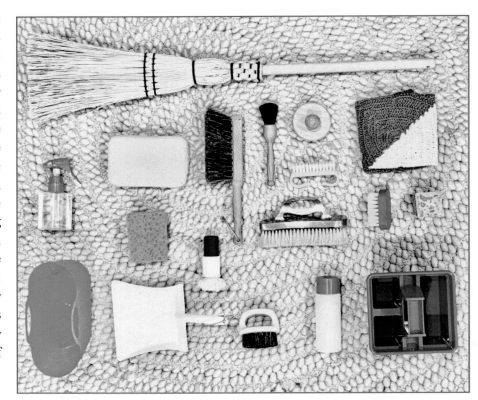

Family Meals Wrap-Up

Family meals, whether at home, with extended family or friends, or out at a restaurant, are essential to the life of your family. Helping children to have different responsibilities for the meal aids their understanding of all the parts that go into a meal. Children who grow up contributing to family meals understand what it takes to care for themselves, to care for others, and to care for their community. They know they can make a contribution and feel purpose in their actions. Family meals keep us connected, no matter the makeup of our family. All families look different, share different customs, and have their own expectations. And all families have the capacity to create strong individuals and relationships through preparing and sharing food.

— Part III —
Special Considerations

"The discovery of a new dish does more for the happiness of the human race than the discovery of a star."

— Jean Anthelme Brillat-Savarin

A Well-Developed Palate:
Breaking the Picky-Eater Habit

"If this is coffee, please bring me some tea; but if this is tea, please bring me some coffee."

— Abraham Lincoln

A young child won't starve himself. I can't tell you how often I reassure parents of this fact. Humans are programmed to meet their own need for nourishment. A newborn baby searches for a nipple just through his sense of smell. And a hungry child will always eat. Many families I work with have "picky eaters." I believe this to be true. Children do pick and choose what they want to eat and in a culture of abundance, we often give too many choices for a young child.

The foods you enjoy now might be somewhat different than the foods you enjoyed as a child. Learning to taste and enjoy new foods comes with practice, experience, and exposure. It is possible to not like a food when you first try it and then come to love the taste and texture over time. It is also possible to prefer a food with a certain combination of other foods, rather than just on its own (think cranberry sauce). Our food preferences evolve throughout our lives. The only way for this to evolve is to not allow ourselves to hold a belief that we do not like a particular food.

The same is true for your child. If he refuses a food or says he doesn't like it, allow him to have this opinion, but try not to give it much attention. Instead, respect his choice not to eat it. This is the moment to allow him to refuse, try not to convince him to try it, and do not offer to replace it with a food you know he prefers.

I hear from many parents who are concerned about their children being picky eaters. In order for a child to like a variety of foods, he must try a range of foods repeatedly. A discerning palate takes time to develop through experience. A child may not like a food the first time he tastes it, but that does not mean he won't come to love that food with time and repeated exposure. If a child is hungry, he will eat what is available. If you offer healthful choices, your child will eat and be nourished. Aside from some health issues, children feel hungry and eat. If you think your child may have a health issue related to eating, consult your pediatrician.

Young children are naturally drawn to consistency and order. They like routine and they like to know what to count on. Earlier in the book, we discussed that consistent expectations lead to a feeling of safety. This is true for most of a young child's life and is also true in their preferences in food. If a child has found a food they prefer, it feels predictable and safe to have that food at every meal. It is your responsibility as a parent to help your child to feel safe while they keep trying new foods. This can be done by creating a consistent routine in how you offer new foods and a consistent environment in which your child eats. For more on a consistent environment read the section Choosing Dishes, Furniture, and Tools.

To create a consistent routine, and create an atmosphere for your child to be comfortable with trying new foods, he needs a few things from you:

1. <u>Provide opportunities to try new food:</u> Just because he pushes food away or says he doesn't like a food, that doesn't mean you should never offer it again. Don't make a big deal about his refusal and offer it again in the near future. This is especially important for very young children.

2. <u>Model trying new food:</u> When he sees that you are willing to try something new, he will also see that he can try (and enjoy!) new foods. Make sure that you try new foods in a natural way at a meal. Make a subtle comment about the taste. There is no need to put on a dramatic show about trying something new. Treat it like it is an everyday occurrence.

3. <u>Take your time and be patient:</u> It may take your child time to learn to like new foods. Often young children have a strong sense of order and trying something new may disturb this. When you make trying something new a regular experience for him, it will become part of his routine.

4. <u>Keep the pressure low:</u> When a new food is offered, serve yourself in a very matter-of-fact way. Pass the food to your child and enjoy your food in a natural way. Sometimes when we draw too much attention to something new it adds unneeded pressure to the situation.

If You Already Have a Picky Eater, Consider the Following

- <u>Children may be sensitive to food texture:</u> You may find that your child is actually more sensitive to the texture of foods than to the taste of food. Try the same flavor in a different consistency; smoother, chunkier, finger foods...

- <u>A child may need repeated offers of a new food:</u> A child may refuse a food at one meal. This does not mean they will not come to like this food in the future. Offer this food whenever you prepare it.

- <u>A child has made a habit of waiting:</u> A child may seem to "hold-out" for their favorite foods. However, a child cannot choose an item if it is not offered.   Although they may try, you can always say, "I hear you asking for yogurt, but yogurt is not a choice right now."   Create (and maintain) an agreement that the food that is prepared for the family is the food that is available to your child. Creating separate meals of everyone's favorite undermines unity in the family and the feeling of a shared meal (plus, making many different dishes is exhausting). I like to use the rule, one family, one meal.

- <u>Healthful food is always available:</u>   Place a basket of fruits on a low shelf in the kitchen with a stack of small napkins next to it. Choose a couple of fruits that your child can eat independently and leave them within his reach. You can also do this with individual containers of crackers or other small snacks, making sure that the snacks are always a healthy choice, and you do not put out more than you want him to eat in a day.   The rule to institute here is: Always sit at the table when you are eating. If he gets up from his table, ask him to put the food away, if he refuses, take the food away and tell him the food will be available later when he is ready to sit at the table and eat. The limit helps him learn your family culture. If he does not follow this rule and also refuses to eat, he may be trying to control the situation. Young children try to control their environment when they feel out of control. If this is the case for your child, try giving him control in other areas of his life such as activities in the day, dressing, and participating in family life. Having the option to choose healthful snacks is one more opportunity for your child to feel he has some control in his life; choice within limits.

- <u>Children learn to self-regulate:</u> Children are able to self-regulate, and when we give them opportunities to practice this, they can more quickly adopt self-regulation into their self-knowledge. Understanding the feelings within their body such as a growling stomach, a full bladder, or a pain in the ear, can all help a child to express his needs and start to meet those needs independently. Picky eaters may not be in touch with these feelings yet. If your child is not in touch with these feelings and they rely on you to tell them when to eat or how many bites to eat, they are not developing the skill to listen to their own body signals. If your child says he is not hungry, honor that statement and offer the same healthful meal later. Repeat this throughout the day always offering the healthful meal, and not resorting to his favorite foods in an attempt to get him to eat something. He will eat when he is hungry. He will learn that when he is hungry, the food that is available will satisfy his hunger.

- <u>Company is always better:</u> A child will sit longer at the table and often eat more when someone sits with him. He will stay even longer if that person is also eating. It is the natural social nature of humans.

Young children have food preferences (just like adults do!), and depending on their personality, they may or may not be adventurous in trying new foods. Although your child may seem picky at the moment, this moment does not define who she is or who she will always be. Continue to offer variety, model trying new foods, and do not panic. She will try new foods, unless you train yourself to only cater to a picky eater.

Often when young children feel out of control, they try to control one or both of two aspects of their life: eating and toileting. Feeling out of control for a young child usually comes when the adults in their life live around them, rather than with them. "Living around" means that all the decisions are made without including your child. It is not essential that your child make the choices for the family, but it can be helpful if his input is asked for and valued in some aspects.

Choices a young child can make:

- To go to the park or play in the back yard

- To have spaghetti or rotini for dinner

- To purchase Roma or Beefsteak tomatoes

- To wear a red shirt or a blue shirt

Offering choices like these allows you to control the general nature of the situation while empowering your child to participate in family life. Giving your child more control of his life may help him feel more willing to participate in family meals.

Other events that may affect your child's feeling of control include:

- Going on vacation

- Moving

- Gaining a sibling

- A death in the family

- Parents schedule changing

- Starting school or daycare

No, Thank You

"I know what I want. I want it all. I want to try everything once."
— Anthony Bourdain

If you find that you are living with a picky eater and need to start a process to get out of the rut of mac n' cheese and chicken nuggets, start the "no-thank-you-bite" rule. The "no-thank-you-bite" rule states that you do not have to like a food, but everyone at the table must take a bite before they can say "no, thank you." By creating this rule where you try a food before turning it down, you build a pattern of trying a new food. A child must decide to not eat more after he has tasted it, and it may be that one day, he tastes something he likes. This also exposes him to more textures and gustatory experiences.

On Being Vegetarian

"Eat food. Not too much. Mostly plants."

— Michael Pollan

My family is a vegetarian family. My husband and I were vegetarian before we had children and decided we wanted to keep the diet and lifestyle with children. We maintain a healthful diet for our family while adhering to a non-meat diet. We're not nutritionists. We're not pushy about other people changing to a vegetarian diet. The truth is that we rarely talk about it, even with our kids. It's just how we live. For us, it's simple. For our kids, it's simple. We don't make a big deal about it.

When we do discuss it with our children it is usually within the context of discussing meal planning and all the parts to a nutritious meal. When we discuss protein options, we discuss the many possibilities of plant based proteins. When they have asked about meat that others are eating or purchasing from the market, we matter-of-factly state what it is called and from which animal it comes.

Here are a few reflections on how we maintain our vegetarian diet:

1. <u>Always name what you are eating and don't call it something it is not.</u> If you are eating a soy protein nugget that is shaped to look like a chicken nugget, do not call it chicken. Or as they are often labeled "Chik'n". Calling non-animal protein by animal names will make it difficult and confusing for your child when she is navigating food choices in your absence.

2. <u>Offer variety and do not restrict yourself by preferences.</u> We all have preferences. I love fruit and cheese and would live on only those if it were possible. (Okay, there would be some wine and chocolate too!) It is important that I continue to offer a variety of foods even if my child claims he doesn't like them. Children's taste in food changes over time, just as it can for adults. It is the continued openness to trying food that allows a child to expand his palate. If he refuses to eat, let it go, don't make it an issue. He will eat with time. Children need different amounts of food and that often changes as they grow. Once your child is eating the same meal as you and you are sitting together daily for family meals, challenge yourself to try a new fruit or vegetable each week.

In time, your child will have a greater understanding of the variety of edible plants in the world. They will also have a diverse vocabulary to go with it (bonus)!

3. Offer balanced meals. A balanced diet includes healthy fats, carbohydrates, fruits, vegetables, and protein. Vegetarians get proteins from many sources including plant based proteins such as quinoa, lentils, soy beans, legumes, nuts, greens, and animal products such as eggs and dairy.

4. Offer healthful snacks. It seems that our children need snacks in-between meals. Vegetarians need as much protein as people who eat meat: 2 oz (56 g) a day for 2-3 year-olds; 4 oz (113 g) for 4-8 year-olds; and 5 oz (141 g) for 9-18 year-olds.[4] It may take a larger portion of plants to get that amount of protein so healthful snacks may be needed. For example, ¼ cup (50 g) of cooked beans, two tablespoons (30 g) of hummus, or ½ ounce (15 g) of nuts are each equivalent to 1 oz (30 g) of cooked chicken or beef.[5] In order to help satisfy this need, at our house we keep a bowl of fruits and vegetables available as well as easy access to nuts and hummus for snacking when the children are hungry. This keeps healthy fiber in their diet and allows them to satisfy their own hunger.

5. Minimize consumption of processed foods. I know many vegetarians who feel limited in ideas about what to eat. It can be easy to resort to processed crackers, granola bars, and other snacks that contain high levels of sodium, dyes, and preservatives that are not healthful. Try keeping roasted almonds and dried fruit handy if you are in need of a snack or a sugar boost.

Dining Out

Many parents dread going out to dinner with a young child because they are afraid that their child will cause a scene. It is always a possibility that your child may become upset; we cannot predict everything that could happen. However, you can prepare for many possibilities.

1. Practice: Having sit-down dinners at home is a preparation for eating at a restaurant. Each time you sit down as a family for a meal at home, you are practicing for your next meal out as a family.

2. Bring a set of dishes: It may be helpful to bring your child-size plate, glass, and flatware that your child uses at home. Restaurants do not often have these items available, making it difficult for your child to fully participate in the meal.

3. Invite your child to be a part of the process: Take the opportunity to introduce pictures on the menu or new words. Discuss options with your child and then give him two to choose from. Even pre-verbal children can suggest preferences with facial expressions and hand gestures.

4. Choose your seating wisely: Make sure to be seated in a way that your child can see people or look outside. Check that he won't get overwhelmed and that he is not facing a screen.

5. Ask for your meals to be served together: Many restaurants assume that children should be served first. The difficulty with this is, when a child finishes eating just as the parents' meals arrive, the child is ready to move onto the next activity and the parent hasn't eaten. This often results in one parent taking the child outside while the other eats alone. This is no fun. A purpose of a family meal out is to eat together, therefore, everyone should be served at the same time.

In order to maximize the possibility of an enjoyable family meal out, keep in mind the time of day—is your child usually getting ready for sleep at this time? Consider his activity of the day—has it been a full day of activity (this might just be too much to ask)? What about his level of hunger? Is your child hungry enough for food to keep his attention, or is he over-hungry and asking him to wait is not going to work? All of these will factor into his ability to sit and enjoy a meal while out.

Over-Eating

From the time you first offer solid food, you can watch your child's signs for being full. He may turn his head away from the food or wiggle his body because of the feeling of a full stomach. Young children may get up from the table or even throw food when they are finished eating. When he signals he is full, stop offering food. If you continue to feed him or try to negotiate ("Just two more bites") you suggest that he does not know the feeling he has within his own body. You are asking him to ignore his body's signal of being full. However, there may be times that he is actually not full and wants more food. How do you navigate this situation? It can be tricky. A young child is working on impulse control and it can be difficult as a parent to recognize when a child simply wants to play with a toy he just saw, or is feeling full and therefore finished eating.

As a parent, this is something you are trying to figure out from the moment your child is born. If you are a nursing mother, you learn to trust that your body is producing the food your baby needs to thrive. For bottle-feeding families, you have a greater focus on the number of ounces consumed. Focussing on the amount can take your attention away from observing your child's signals. Understanding your child's signs will help you know when to offer food and when to stop offering food. If you are feeding your child and they show you signs that they are full. Respect those signals, stop offering food, and offer again later. The amount of food your child needs can change from day to day. By responding to his signals you allow him to experience the consequences of signaling he is finished.

The American Academy of Pediatrics and the CDC list the following:

Signs your infant may be hungry:

• Puts hands to mouth

• Turns head towards mom's breast or bottle

• Puckers, smacks, or licks lips

• Has clenched hands

Don't Hide the Veggies

So many parents I talk with are concerned about their child rejecting vegetables. I have heard of many ways to sneak vegetables into recipes. However, it is important for your child to know what he is eating. This is not only important language and sensorial information, but a way to build trust with your child. Help him to understand what goes into his food. He may not like it the first time he tries it, but keep offering it over the next week or so. For foods that he consistently rejects, offer it every once in a while. Make sure not to create expectations by saying, "I know you didn't like these beans last time, but we are going to try again." Simply say, "I roasted some beans for us to eat today." There will be some foods that he just doesn't like. When it is so early in developing his palate, it is important to keep offering a variety of vegetables. Preferences change over time and food may be rejected for flavor or texture. Sometimes it is less about an individual food and may be a combination.

Signs your infant may be full:

• Closes mouth

• Turns head away from mom's breast or bottle

• Relaxes hands

Signs your young child may be hungry:

• Reaches for or points to food

• Opens their mouth when offered a spoon or food

• Gets excited when they see food

• Uses hand motions or sounds for food to let you know they are still hungry

Signs your young child may be full:

• Pushes food away

• Closes their mouth when food is offered

• Turns their head away from food

• Uses hand motions or sounds for food to let you know they are full[6]

In order for a person to respond to their own needs, they need to be aware of their body, how to take care of it, and the signals their body gives. This is very similar to potty learning. There is no way for a parent to know 100% when a child needs to empty his bladder. It is through watching your child's behaviors and routine and responses to his feelings that you learn. This is the same for anticipating when your child is hungry and full. Watch for signals. If your child signals that he is full, respect that, remove the food and if you suspect he is still hungry, offer again in the near future. Help him to learn to self regulate.

When Eating Patterns Change

It seems, in parenting, just when you have figured out a pattern or a system that works, things change. Your child has a growth spurt, your mother comes to visit, or your refrigerator stops working and then everything in life shifts. It can be so frustrating! The following is a list of common times when your child's eating patterns may change. Remember, consistency and routine are your friends (but not rigidity—rigidity is not your friend) and they will see you through most of these times.

1. <u>When there's a growth spurt - cognitive or physical.</u> Often just before a growth spurt, children eat more. This is their way of feeding the brain and body in advance of a big leap. A growth spurt may be that a child is getting taller or gaining weight. It can also be a cognitive connection that is not always perceivable. Your child may suddenly make an intellectual connection—an understanding or awareness of his world he did not previously have. Another form of a physical growth spurt is the acquisition of a new skill such as crawling, or pulling-to-standing, or a refinement of movement such as the ability to use two hands to hold a toy or using a pincer grasp with his fingers.

2. <u>When he is busy moving (crawling, pulling up, walking).</u> Children who are focussed on movement and are new to the ability to locomote, may not want to take the time to stop and eat. Often this is a temporary focus. A baby who wants to move and doesn't seem to stop may all of a sudden notice that he is very hungry and may eat in a hurry or feel the hunger and quickly become upset. This is because he is focussed on movement and doesn't notice his hunger until it is all consuming. Then, to her, it seems quite urgent. If this happens with your little one, help her to take the time to slow down and sit at the table to eat. Many parents may find themselves worried about their child's nutrition and start to follow their child around putting food in their child's mouth any chance they get. This creates bad habits around eating and is a choking hazard for the child. Eating is its own activity and should not be encouraged to be a part of movement activities.

3. <u>When he feels out of control.</u> Young children control very few decisions in their lives. When they are feeling that life is happening around them and everything is too fast to understand, he may stop eating. This is one thing he can control. Other things he may try to control include when and where he urinates or has bowel movements. Young children benefit from feeling in control of some aspects of their life. If you find your child is feeling that he wants more control, you can offer more choices throughout the day.

Choices that are low-stress and beneficial to a young child's ownership of his experiences include:

• choosing clothing to wear

• choosing produce at the grocery store

• choosing between plants to water in the yard

• choosing which bath toys to add to the bath

• choosing to add bubbles or not in his bath

• choosing a color of towel to use.

These are all examples that matter very little in the grand scheme of decisions in family life. However, for a young child, they can be the difference of feeling included in family life or not.

4. When she is not hungry. There are actually times when your child is not hungry. It may be that she has had regular feeding times for a while, and then one day she is just not hungry at that time. Respect her refusal to eat and offer food later in the day. It is important not to try to manipulate your child into eating by bribing her. Another mistake parents often make is to keep offering different foods until they name one that the child says yes to. This is a dangerous pattern as it sends the message that if she waits long enough, her favorite food will be offered. We all have food preferences, but it is helpful to try new foods, eat diverse foods, and be open to new gustatory experiences. Children who are catered to are more likely to become the dreaded "picky eater". Children who are offered a healthy meal and refuse it will experience that healthy food is available when he is hungry. He will then learn to appreciate his body signals and a variety of food.

5. When she doesn't feel well. When children are not well, their appetite may be suppressed. It is important to keep your little one hydrated, even though she may not eat much solid food until she is feeling better. Children who are still nursing may ask to nurse more since the nursing relationship and milk are comforting.

If you are concerned that your child may not be getting enough nutrition from their meals, talk with your pediatrician.

Food Sensitivity Substitutions

If you or your child has food allergies or sensitivities to ingredients, you may want ti make substitutions in food preparation. This may just be temporary as your child's digestive system matures. If you are concerned about food allergies, you should talk with your pediatrician. This chart shows some simple substitutions you can make in baking recipes.

Food	Substitute	How much
Cow's Milk	Goat, Soy, Rice, Coconut Milk, or water	Equal amount
Egg	Applesauce or mashed banana	¼ cup (60 ml) per egg
Butter	Olive Oil or coconut oil	¾ cup (180 ml) oil to 1 cup (225 g) butter
Butter	Margarine	Equal amount
Wheat flour	Brown Rice flour, chickpea flour, coconut flour, or a combination	Equal amount
Nut butter	Sunbutter, soy butter	Equal amount
Sugar	Maple syrup, agave nectar, mashed banana	½ cup (120 ml) to 1 cup (200 g) sugar

III. Special Considerations

— Part IV —
Recipes for Families

"I don't know what it is about food your mother makes for you, especially when it's something that anyone can make - pancakes, meat loaf, tuna salad - but it carries a certain taste of memory."

— Mitch Albom

A Few Basics

In order to cook for or with your child, there are a few items that are required and many that are suggested. Food preparation does not have to include cooking and some of our recipes do not require a heat element at all. The items at hand in your kitchen may look or have a name different from what is listed below.

Required for most Recipes:

- Oven/Stovetop
- Sink
- Tray
- Large Mixing Bowl - choose one with a rubber bottom or a handle to stabilize while mixing
- Measuring cups
- Measuring spoons
- Cutting board and knife
- Mixing spoon or spatula

Recommended to maximize a child's independence and help make cooking with your child go more smoothly:

- Stool to work at counter height
- Child-size apron
- Small convection oven
- Vegetable steamer/rice cooker
- Parchment paper
- Six small bowls
- Two small pitchers
- Bowl for compost
- Low water access or sink
- Low table and chair
- Towels and sponge for clean-up

Recipes

1. Recipes for First Meals

2. Recipes To Prepare Collaboratively With Your Child

3. Recipes for Your Child To Prepare Independently

- Basic Recipes

- Advanced Recipes

Recipes for First Meals

Pear Purée

Roasted Sweet Potatoes

Egg Yolk

Steamed Garlic and Ginger Carrots

This section gives you a start in preparing food for your baby's first meals. There are many combinations of food you can offer once you begin the weaning process. Here are a few things to keep in mind when choosing what to offer:

1. If you have any concerns about food allergies, talk to your pediatrician *before* introducing solid foods.

2. Make sure each solid food meal is a complete meal with protein, healthy fats, carbohydrates, fruits, vegetables, and water.

3. Serve small amounts on the plate in front of your child at the table. Leave the full serving in a serving dish (out of his reach). If your child finishes the food on the plate, add more to his plate from the serving dish.

4. Place a spoon with a small amount of food on his plate. Then feed him with another spoon. He will try to pick up the spoon on his plate and bring it to his mouth, while you feed him small bites. This is how he learns to feed himself and be an active participant in his meals. You will be amazed at how this works!

5. A typical serving for one meal is about one to two tablespoons (14-30 g) per food. Consider preparing larger portions at a time and then freezing the extra in silicone ice cube or muffin trays. Once they are frozen pop them into a labeled airtight container and keep them in the freezer for up to three months.

6. Follow the solid food meal with breastmilk or formula. Your child may tire of eating before he is full. Following with milk will allow him to complete his meal. It is important to not start with milk as he may fill up before he begins his solid food. As he eats more solid food, he will need less milk.

7. Choose one new food each week to add to your child's meal options. This will give your child time to get used to the new flavor and texture, and allow you to take note of any possible reactions.

8. Only purée food for the first couple of weeks, then transition to a slightly chunkier texture so your child can get used to the new texture and learn to use his jaw to chew.

9. Babies love tasty food. When you cook for your child, use the same herbs and spices you use in your own cooking.

Pear Purée

Makes 4-6 servings

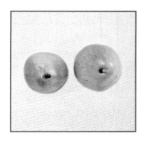 

Ingredients

2 organic pears
3 tablespoons (45 ml) water

Preparation

1. Peel, core, and cube the pears.
2. Over medium heat, in a saucepan, bring water and pears to a slow simmer.
3. When pears are tender (about 10 minutes), remove from heat.
4. Allow the pears and water to cool.
5. Use a food processor to purée pears and water.

Tip!

Purchase very ripe pears and skip the cooking. Fresh pears can be peeled, cored and puréed.

Roasted Sweet Potatoes

Makes 6-8 servings

Ingredients

2 organic sweet potatoes

2 tablespoons (30 ml) organic olive oil

2 teaspoons (5 g) cinnamon

Preparation

1. Preheat the oven to 375°F (190°C).
2. Peel and cube the potatoes.
3. Spread the potato cubes in single layer on a baking sheet lined with parchment paper.
4. Drizzle olive oil over the potato cubes.
5. Sprinkle cinnamon over potato cubes.
6. Bake at 375°F (190°C) for 25-30 minutes until tender.
7. Remove and allow to cool to room temperature.
8. Use a fork to mash the potato cubes into a smooth purée.

Tip!

Use a smoother texture for first meals and change to chunkier textures as your child gets older. Eventually, you can serve the cubes of potatoes as is and your child will use a fork or his pincer grasp to feed himself.

Egg Yolk

Makes 1 serving (this should always be made fresh, not frozen)

Ingredients

1 egg
Breastmilk, or other non-dairy milk to create desired consistency

Preparation

1. Hard boil the egg.
2. Allow egg to cool to room temperature.
3. Remove egg shell and egg white.
4. Use a fork to mash the egg yolk and combine with the breastmilk until the texture is smooth.

Steamed Garlic and Ginger Carrots

Makes 6-8 Servings

Ingredients

6 organic carrots

1 clove of organic garlic

1 teaspoon (2.5 g) ground ginger

Preparation

1. Peel and slice the carrots into disks.
2. Peel the garlic clove.
3. Steam carrots and garlic for 10 minutes, until carrots are tender.
4. Remove the garlic clove.
5. Sprinkle the carrots with ginger.
6. Allow the carrots to cool to room temperature.
7. Use a fork to mash the carrots into a smooth purée.

Tip!

Use a smoother texture for first meals and change to chunkier textures as your child gets older. Eventually, you can serve the slices as is and your child will use a fork or his pincer grasp to feed himself.

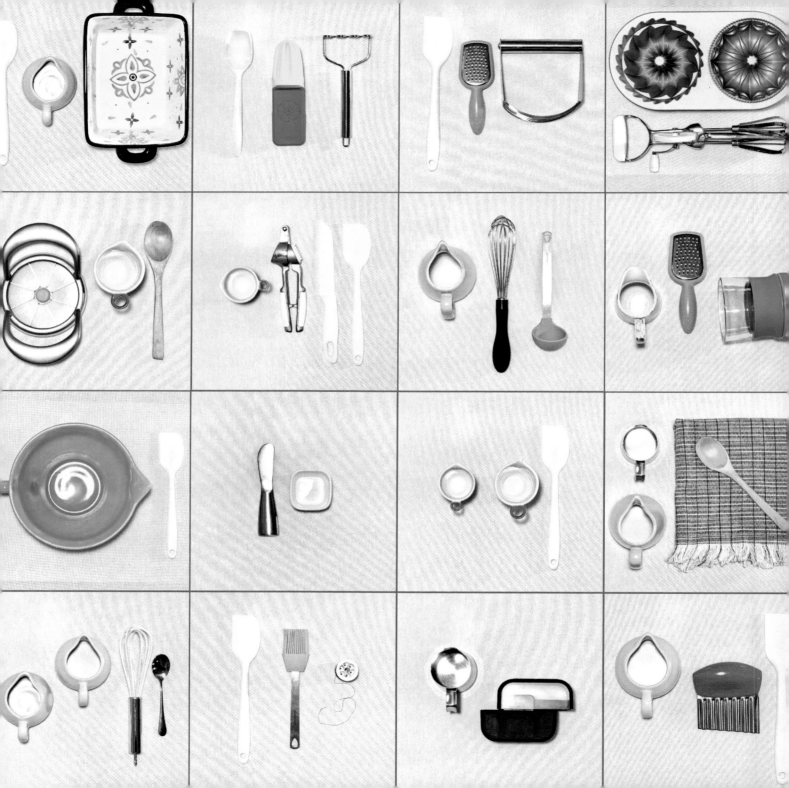

Recipes To Prepare Collaboratively With Your Child

Roasted Beans With Butter And Garlic

Roasted squash

Baked apples

Vegan Ranch Dip

Cheesy Rice Casserole

Granola

Cornbread

Banana Muffins

Popovers

Vegan Tortilla Soup

Bread

Cinnamon rolls

Preparing To Cook With Your Child

Children can start preparing food with you as soon as they are eating solid foods and can coordinate their two hands together. Consider waiting until your child is no longer exploring orally before introducing food preparation. Children will occasionally taste food while preparing. That's fine, however, it is best to encourage your child to wait until the food is served to eat it.

When preparing your materials for working with your child, or for them to prepare food independently, there are a few developmental steps we should consider. First, consider your child's natural sense of order. Children long to understand the routine and systems in their life. They love knowing what to anticipate next; laying out materials and ingredients in order of use from left to right and top to bottom allows for this predictability. Regularity and consistency allow a child to be more independent in her life, especially when it comes to food preparation.

It is easy to see children's love of order when they make sure to place their shoes just so when they put them away, when they display their toys in ordered rows on their shelf (they especially like to do this with action figures and cars), or in their display of their self-care objects in the bathroom such as a toothbrush, a hairbrush, and a container of lotion. The other natural tendency that is important to recognize is children's love of presentation and beautification. This natural love helps a child become aware of presentation and attention to detail. When we acknowledge and prepare to support this tendency a child feels welcome in this space. A space designed to accommodate a child's needs, creativity, and preferences offers opportunity for intellectual growth.

A Montessori approach acknowledges the human desire to see a beautiful presentation and the need to be able to present something in a beautiful way. A child demonstrates this when they when they carefully place a flower arrangement on the table or draw pictures in the margins of their writing. This is visible in all children, but as it may not match your own preferences, it may take stepping back and observing to see their unique view and style.

Working successfully alongside your child in the kitchen takes preparation, patience, practice, and the ability to live in the moment. In order to have a successful and rewarding experience, here are my best tips for working side-by-side with a young child in the kitchen:

1. Read the recipe ahead of time and measure and prepare ingredients before you tell your child what you are preparing

2. Use a sturdy stool or Kitchen Helper™ to bring your child up to the counter height. Alternatively, you can sit together at a low table to prepare the food.

3. Always wash your hands as your child washes his hands before you begin and keep a towel close by for wiping hands as you go if needed. Some children do not like the feeling of messy hands. For this child, it will be important to have a damp towel near by so they can wipe their hands as often as they like.

4. Set out the ingredients from left to right and top to bottom. (See our tray images in the following recipes for examples.)

5. Introduce the recipe by naming the item you are making. Then name each ingredient. Take time to smell and touch the ingredients. Remember, this is an important part of the experience for both sensorial exploration and language development.

6. Always show how to do a step and then give your child a turn. First, show your child how to do the step. For example, say, "We need to add the flour to the mixing bowl." Then pour a small amount of flour from its bowl into the mixing bowl. Set the flour bowl down and ask your child if they would like to add the flour. Do this for each step until your child starts to understand the motor control needed to manage the tools and ingredients. With practice, your child will understand that each ingredient is added in order. You will eventually be able to ask your child to add an ingredient without demonstrating first.

7. Remember it is the experience that is more valuable to your child than the final product. Try not to focus on whether the food will 'look good' when you are done, it is the process of the activity that teaches young children about what goes into their food. Someday they will take notice and also put effort into a beautiful finished product. Let that come from them naturally.

8. Clean up as you go along with the recipe; wipe up big spills as they happen, don't fuss about the little spills. Keep a wet cloth nearby to help with little spills; larger ones might require a pause in the activity to clean up. Cleaning is part of the process and helps your child understand that when mistakes happen, we calmly take care of it and move forward.

9. Acknowledge your child's efforts rather than passing judgement. While cooking with your child consider making comments like, "You are stirring very consistently; that will make for a smooth batter." Avoid empty praise like, "Good job!" or "Good girl!" Give feedback on what they are doing to prepare food well and your child will feel pride with your acknowledgement. This is also something that you can do when you sit together to eat the food. Children feel proud when you eat together and mention, "These muffins we made are tasty," or "Thank you for slicing the fruit for our fruit salad."

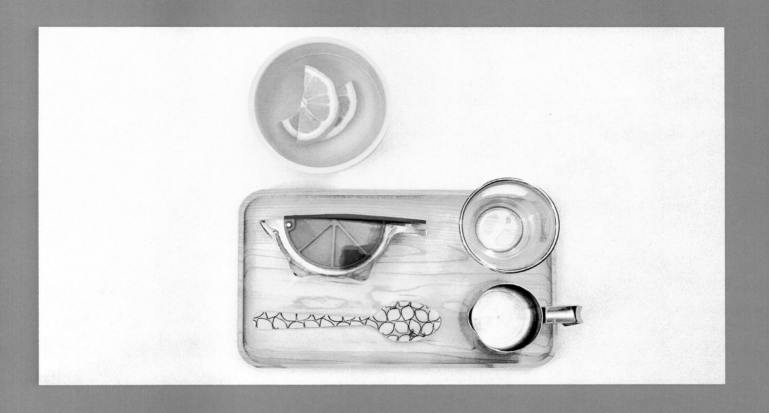

It is almost possible to say that there is a mathematical relationship between the beauty of his surroundings and the activity of the child; he will make discoveries rather more voluntarily in a gracious setting than in an ugly one.

— Maria Montessori

The first recipes in this section describe the parts the adult should do and then the parts the child can do. As you progress through this section, we leave more of these choices up to you. The more you cook with your child, the more you will know what to help with and when to step back. If you feel you have stepped back too far, it is always possible to reinsert yourself and say, "I will help with this part, and you will get a turn." Children understand taking turns and are usually happy to trade off with you.

The Perfect Tray

The photos in this section of the book are meant to help you visualize how to set up a tray for a young chef. The materials are pre-measured and set out clearly in the tray in order of use—left to right and top to bottom. Keeping consistency in order helps your child internalize how to follow these visual cues.

Many of the dishes from recipe to recipe are reused. It is not necessary to have a huge collection of small dishes. A set of six small bowls, two small pitchers, and one mixing bowl will be sufficient for most recipes.

Hand-Over-Hand

Sometimes young children can learn how to use tools by adults offering hand-over-hand guidance. In order for children to develop controlled and purposeful movement, it helps if they can see and feel the movement step-by-step, and more slowly than we would normally do the movement. Because they may not yet understand what it means when we say, "stir the batter," it may help to put your hand gently on top of your child's hand and make large circles with the mixing spoon in the batter. As you do this, your child can feel the large arm movement it takes to mix. After you do this a couple of times, your child usually can manage on their own.

Some children refuse hand-over-hand instruction. Whether it is unwanted touch or a strong desire to do things on their own, some children are not open to it. In this case, it is important to show clearly how to stir. Tell your child, "I will show you how to stir, and then you will get a turn." Be deliberate and slow in your arm movement. As

Knolling

Knolling is the organization and layout of tools or similar items in an interesting way; usually in parallel and perpendicular ways. Knolling is the way we create trays and activities for a child to use and be successful in their work. In many of the photos in this book you will see knolling as a way to illustrate the order of ingredients and tools for recipes. Children are drawn to order and beauty. Knolling incorporates both of these to create an interesting activity that is purposeful and easy to follow. Knolling supports the child's success in food preparation, baking, and almost any activity we set out for them.

The Easy Way – Use a Mix!

Creating these layouts can be overwhelming for some. If this is the case for you, focus on the experience of cooking with your child and let go of being 100% precise with these recipes and layouts. If you are looking to cook with your child but are not ready to build tray layouts or multi-step recipes, start with a store-bought mix. Choose a muffin mix that just requires adding water. These are usually available in small packets or boxes in the baking aisle in the grocery store. These mixes offer a way to support your family in preparing food together without the stress. When my children were younger, I kept a couple of these in my pantry so if my child had a need to contribute to a meal and I did not have the time or energy to prepare a recipe from scratch, I would pull one of these out and we were all set!

you stir do not speak. Let them watch without the disruption of words. Then, invite your child to have a turn. If needed, repeat this until your child slows down and mixes in large circles. If he refuses to mix slowly, you can say, "I see you are having a difficult time keeping all the ingredients in the bowl. I will finish mixing and next time you will get another turn." By doing this, you set the limit that your child can participate as well as appreciate his need for independence, and you will preserve the integrity of the activity and not allow him to waste the ingredients.

Roasted Beans With Butter and Garlic

Makes 6-8 servings

Ingredients

1 lb (500 g) fresh green beans

3 tablespoons (45 g) unsalted butter, melted

1 clove of garlic

Materials

Strainer

Towel

Large bowl

Compost bowl

4 oz (125 ml) pitcher for the melted butter

Bowl for garlic clove

Garlic shredder or press

Baking sheet lined with parchment paper

Preparation

1. Preheat the oven to 400°F (205°C)

2. Show your child how to hold the strainer with green beans under the running water in the sink. Show him how to move the beans and wash the beans in the water.

3. Place the strainer on a towel on work surface (table or counter).

4. Show your child how to snap off the ends of a bean and place the ends in the compost bowl.

5. Place the bean in the large bowl.

6. *Optional:* if you want the beans smaller, after both the ends are snapped off, show your child how to snap the beans in half and then to place them in the large bowl.

7. Continue until all the beans are snapped.

8. Set the large bowl aside and show your child how to place the garlic clove in the shredder and how to use the shredder. Invite your child to repeat shredding the garlic.

9. Place the shredded garlic in a bowl with the melted butter. Set aside.

10. Invite your child to place the beans in a single layer on the lined baking sheet.

11. Show him how to drizzle the butter on the beans. Invite him to repeat.

12. Roast the beans at 400°F for 15 minutes.

13. Remove and serve warm.

Roasted Squash Noodles

Makes 8-10 servings

Ingredients

1 butternut squash

4 tablespoons (60 ml) olive oil

2 teaspoons (5 g) cinnamon

1 whole nutmeg

Materials

Small bowls for each ingredient

Spiralizer

Pitcher or oil dispenser for oil

Mini grater

Baking sheet lined with parchment paper

Preparation

1. Preheat the oven to 450°F (230°C)

2. Use the spiralizer to make squash noodles as per the instructions that come with your machine. Show your child how to use it and then invite your child to repeat.

3. Lay the noodles in a single layer on a baking sheet lined with parchment paper.

4. Show your child how to drizzle olive oil over noodles, invite her to repeat.

5. Use the mini grater and show your child how to grate one quarter of the nutmeg into the small bowl.

6. Once the nutmeg is grated, combine with the cinnamon in small bowl.

7. Show your child how to sprinkle this mixture over the noodles. Let him finish the task.

8. Bake at 450°F (230°C) for 10 min.

9. Remove and serve warm.

Baked Apples

Makes 6-8 servings

Ingredients

2 apples, peeled

1 teaspoon (2.5 g) cinnamon

1 tablespoon (15 g) brown sugar

3 tablespoons (45 g) unsalted butter (2 tablespoons melted, 1 tablespoon cold)

Materials

Cutting board

Apple slicer

Knife (for the adult to use)

Small bowls for each ingredient

Small pitcher for melted butter

12 fluid ounce (360 ml) baking dish

Medium mixing bowl

Child-size mixing spoon

Compost bowl

Preparation

1. Preheat the oven to 400°F (205°C)

2. Show your child the apples and explain that you have already removed the peel.

3. Place an apple on the cutting board and slice it in half across the core, creating a top and bottom of the apple.

4. Show your child the seed pattern inside. Ask, "Does that look like a shape you have seen before?" (It's a star!)

5. Slice the second apple in half in the same way.

6. Place the halves back in the bowl.

7. Show your child how to place one half of the apple on the cutting board, flat side down.

8. Show your child how to center the apple slicer on the apple, then start to push down. Invite your child to help you. Repeat with the rest of the apples, placing the apple pieces in the mixing bowl and the core in the compost bowl as you go.

9. Invite your child to pour the melted butter over the apples.

10. Invite your child to sprinkle the cinnamon and brown sugar over the apple slices.

11. Use the mixing spoon to show your child how to mix the apples to coat them with butter, cinnamon, and sugar. Invite your child to have a turn.

12. Using the cold butter, show your child how to rub the entire inside of the baking dish with butter. Invite your child to repeat.

13. Pour the apple mixture into the baking dish.

14. Bake at 400°F (205°C) for 20 minutes.

15. Remove and serve warm.

Vegan Ranch Dip

Makes 8-10 servings

Ingredients

1 clove garlic

¼ cup (6 g) Italian parsley

2 tablespoons (6 g) fresh chives

1 cup (240 g) vegan mayonnaise

½ cup (120 g) vegan sour cream

Splash of soy milk

1 tablespoon (3 g) fresh dill

¼ teaspoon (0.6 g) paprika

1 tablespoon (3 g) fresh oregano

1 teaspoon (5 ml) vegan Worcestershire sauce

Materials

Small bowl for each ingredient

Mixing bowl

Child-size rubber spatula

2 oz (60 ml) pitcher for milk

Garlic press

Child-size serrated acrylic knife

Cutting board

Compost bowl

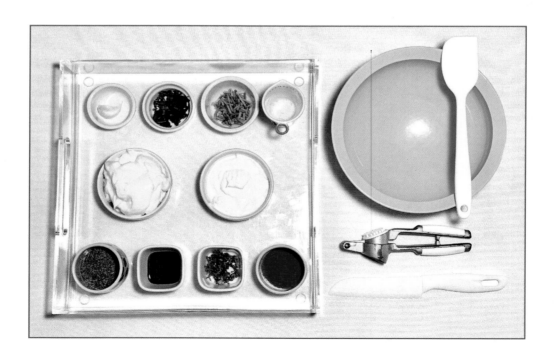

Preparation

1. Show your child the garlic press. Ask your child to put the garlic in the press. Start to press the garlic. Invite your child to have a turn. Finish pressing the garlic if needed.

2. Place the pressed garlic in the mixing bowl.

3. Using the cutting board and knife, show your child how to chop the herbs. Invite her to repeat. Place in mixing bowl. Place any unused stems in the compost bowl.

4. Invite your child to add the remaining ingredients.

5. Mix well.

6. Chill and serve with sliced vegetables.

Cheesy Rice Casserole

Makes 8-10 servings

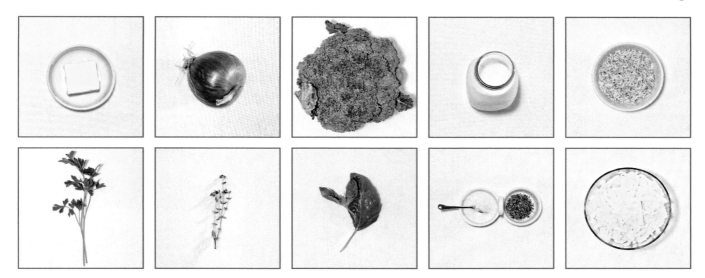

Ingredients

3 tablespoons (45 g) unsalted butter — 2 tablespoons melted and one tablespoon cold

1 small onion, minced

1 head of broccoli

1/4 cup (60 ml) milk

4 cups (800 g) cooked rice

1 teaspoon (1 g) chopped parsley leaves

1 teaspoon (1 g) chopped thyme leaves

1 teaspoon (0.5 g) chopped basil leaves

Salt and pepper (optional, to taste)

2 cups (500 ml or about 225 g) shredded sharp cheddar cheese

Materials

Small bowl for each ingredient

3 oz (100 ml) pitcher for milk

Cutting board

Child-size crinkle knife

3 quart (3 L) baking dish

Compost bowl

Large mixing bowl

Child-size rubber spatula

Aluminum foil

Preparation

1. Preheat the oven to 400°F (205°C)

2. Invite your child to carefully rub the cold butter on the inside of the baking dish.

3. Show your child how to use the crinkle knife and cutting board to cut the broccoli into small pieces. Place stems in the compost bowl.

4. Invite your child to mix milk, 1 1/2 cups of cheese, rice, parsley, thyme, basil, onion, melted butter, and broccoli in large mixing bowl. Mix well.

5. Season with salt and pepper.

6. Work with your child to scoop the mixture into the prepared baking dish.

7. Ask your child to sprinkle the extra shredded cheese over the top of the mixture.

8. Cover with aluminum foil.

9. Bake at 400°F (205°C) for 25 minutes.

10. Remove foil and bake for five more minutes.

11. Remove and serve warm.

Granola

Makes 6-8 servings

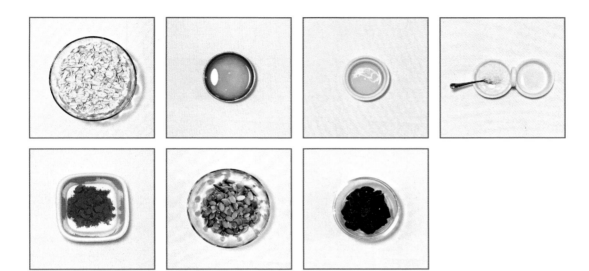

Ingredients

2 cups (180 g) oats

2 tablespoons (30 ml) coconut oil, liquid state

3 tablespoons (45 ml) agave nectar

¼ teaspoon (1.5 g) sea salt

1 teaspoon (2.5 g) cinnamon

⅓ cup (40 g) pumpkin seeds

⅓ cup (65 g) dried fruit, chopped

Materials

Small bowl for each ingredient

3 oz (100 ml) pitcher for oil

3 oz (100 ml) pitcher for agave nectar

Small mixing bowl

Large mixing bowl

Child-size rubber spatula

Baking sheet lined with parchment paper

Preparation

1. Preheat the oven to 325°F (160°C)

2. Invite your child to mix the coconut oil and agave nectar in a small bowl. Set aside.

3. In large bowl ask your child to stir together the oats, salt, cinnamon, and pumpkin seeds.

4. Ask your child to pour the liquid over the dry ingredients. Mix well.

5. Spread the mixture onto baking sheet lined with parchment paper.

6. Bake at 325°F (160°C) for 20-25 minutes, stirring once during this time. (The adult does this step and child watches.)

7. Remove and let cool to room temperature.

8. Place cooked granola into a clean mixing bowl. Invite your child to mix in dried fruit.

9. Serve with milk or store in airtight container.

Cornbread

Makes 6-8 servings

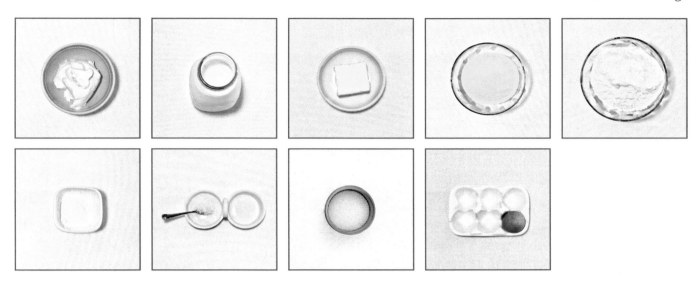

Ingredients

1 cup (250 ml) yogurt

⅓ cup (80 ml) milk

2 tablespoons (30 g) unsalted butter, cold

1 ½ cups (225 g) medium-grind cornmeal

½ cup (60 g) all-purpose flour

1 ½ teaspoon (6 g) baking powder

1 teaspoon (5 g) salt

1 tablespoon (12 g) sugar

1 egg

Materials

Small bowl for each ingredient

4 oz. (120 ml) pitcher for milk

Mixing bowl

Child-size rubber spatula

Compost bowl

12 fluid ounce (360 ml) baking dish

Preparation

1. Preheat the oven to 375°F (190°C).

2. Put the butter in baking dish and place in the pre-heated oven for two minutes. (Your child can put the butter in the dish and you place it in and remove it from the oven.)

3. Invite your child to combine the dry ingredients in the mixing bowl. Mix well.

4. Help your child to crack the egg into the egg bowl. Place the shell in the compost bowl.

5. Ask your child to pour the egg into the mixing bowl and then both you and your child wash your hands. (It is good practice to create a habit of washing hands after touching raw egg.)

6. Invite your child to add the yogurt and mix well.

7. Help your child to pour the batter into the prepared pan. Smooth out the top if necessary.

8. Bake at 375°F (190°C) for 30 minutes, until the top is lightly browned and the sides have pulled away from the pan. A toothpick inserted into the center should come out clean.

9. Remove and serve warm with jam or butter.

Banana Muffins

Makes 6-8 12 muffins

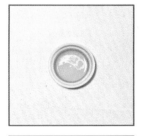    

Ingredients

⅛ cup (30 ml) agave nectar

½ cup (125 ml) vegetable oil

2 eggs

2 small, ripe bananas

1 teaspoon (5 ml) vanilla

1 ⅔ cups (200 g) all-purpose flour

1 teaspoon (6 g) baking soda

½ teaspoon (2.5 g) salt

½ teaspoon (1 g) ground cinnamon

Materials

Small bowl for each ingredient

2 oz (60 ml) pitcher for agave nectar

4 oz (120 ml) pitcher for oil

Compost bowl

Large mixing bowl

Manual hand mixer or whisk

Mini muffin pan prepared with non-stick spray or muffin liners

Child-size spatula

Preparation

1. Preheat oven to 375°F (190°C).

2. Ask your child to pour sugar and oil into the mixing bowl. Beat with manual hand mixer or whisk.

3. Help your child to crack the eggs into the egg bowl. Place the shells in the compost bowl.

4. Ask your child to pour the eggs into the mixing bowl and then both you and your child wash your hands. (It is good practice to create a habit of washing hands when touching raw egg.)

5. Show your child how to squeeze the banana to mash it inside the peel.

6. Invite your child to repeat.

7. Open one end of the banana and squeeze the mash into the mixing bowl. Place banana peel in compost bowl.

8. Ask your child to add the vanilla and mix well.

9. Add each of the remaining ingredients and mix well.

10. Line the muffin pan with paper muffin liners or spray it with non-stick spray.

11. Show your child how to scoop batter with the rubber spatula and pour it into one muffin cup. Invite your child to continue to fill the cups.

12. Bake at 375°F (190°C) for 12 to 15 minutes or until toothpick inserted in center comes out clean.

13. Remove and serve warm.

Popovers

Makes 12-15 popovers

    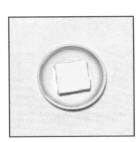

Ingredients

1 cup (120 g) all-purpose flour

¼ teaspoon (1 g) salt

1 cup (250 ml) milk

2 eggs

4 tablespoons (60 g) unsalted butter — 1 tablespoon melted and 3 tablespoons cold, cut into cubes

Materials

Small bowl for each ingredient

8 ounce (250 ml) pitcher for milk

Compost bowl

Mixing bowl

Child-size whisk

Mini popover pan

Child-size ladle

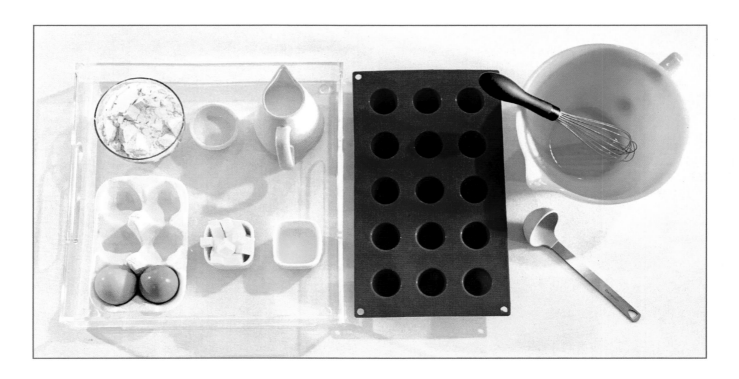

Preparation

1. Preheat oven to 450°F (230°C).

2. Ask your child to place one cube of butter into each division of the popover pan.

3. Place pan in the oven and allow butter to melt. (The adult places and removes the pan in the oven)

4. Once melted, remove the pan from oven and set aside.

5. Invite your child to add the flour and salt to the mixing bowl.

6. Show your child how us the whisk until blended.

7. Ask your child to add the melted butter and milk. Whisk until combined.

8. Help your child to crack the eggs into the egg bowl. Place the shells in the compost bowl.

9. Ask your child to pour the eggs into the mixing bowl and then both you and your child wash your hands. (It is good practice to create a habit of washing hands after touching raw egg.)

10. Using the ladle, show your child how to fill the cups of the prepared popover pan about half full.

11. Bake at 450°F (230°C) for 12-17 minutes until popovers rise.

12. Remove and serve warm with some jam or butter.

There is nothing like soup.
It is by nature eccentric:
no two are ever alike,
unless of course you get your soup in a can.

— Laurie Colwin

Vegan Tortilla Soup

At a first glance this may seem like an overwhelming recipe. However, as you cook more with your child you will learn the balance that works for you in how much you prepare ahead of time and how much you prepare together. When I began cooking with my children, I was not sure how much I could (or should) involve them. Of course, each child had different interests and ability levels. This soup recipe allows for many different levels of participation and independence. This is a recipe you can start when your children are quite young and you can allow more and more independence over time. This is the type of recipe children start to internalize and then later re-create with feeling rather than specific measurements.

This soup is great to make together because there are many things you can do side-by-side (sautéing the onions, pulling the jackfruit, and chopping the toppings) and then there are pieces your child can do independently (slicing avocado, garnishing the bowls for serving, and pouring the broth). I love that this recipe is prepared in separate bowls and the final assembly is done just before eating.

Tip: For young children eating soup, offer a measuring tablespoon instead of a regular spoon as it is often easier for them to use as a scoop.

At the stove with your child

If you determine that your child is ready to work side-by-side with you at the hot stove, allow him to help you stir the sauté as needed. Stay right next to your child during this process; allow him to do only as much as you determine is safe. It may be the case that he watches you do this part from a distance the first time, and then next time he may be ready to help with this part.

Vegan Tortilla Soup

Makes five servings

Ingredients

1 1/2 cups (225 g) canned jackfruit in brine

1 tablespoon (15 ml) olive oil

⅓ cup (50 g) chopped onion

1 clove garlic, minced

5 cups (1.2 L) vegetable broth

1 tablespoon (10 g) roasted hatch pepper

1 cup (200 g) diced tomato

2 teaspoons (4 g) ground cumin

A pinch of salt

1 avocado, sliced

Cilantro, chopped

Tortilla strips

Lime wedges

Materials

Small bowl for each ingredient

Colander

Cutting board

Child-size serrated or crinkle knife

Skillet

Stock pot

Compost bowl

Child-sized spatula

Five 1-cup (250 ml) pitchers for serving

Five soup bowls for serving

Preparation

1. To prepare jackfruit, rinse and drain the fruit in the colander. Cut off the center part of the jackfruit. Pull the stringy part into smaller pieces. Use your hands to pull into small shredded pieces. (Children are great at this part.) Rinse one more time and set aside.

2. Heat olive oil and one tablespoon (15 ml) of broth in skillet over medium heat. Add and sauté the chopped onion and minced garlic. Stir occasionally for 3-5 minutes or until onions are translucent.

3. Add rinsed and shredded jackfruit and sauté for 4-5 minutes. Allow the jackfruit to cook long enough to dry out and brown a bit.

4. Add salt and cumin. Stir.

5. Add 1 tablespoon (15 ml) of vegetable broth to the jackfruit sauté.

6. Reduce heat and simmer for 15 to 20 minutes.

7. Season to taste then remove from heat.

8. Heat the remaining broth in a stock pot over medium heat.

9. To serve, place tortilla strips in serving bowls, top with jackfruit sauté, and garnish with sliced avocado, and chopped cilantro. Place a lime wedge on the side.

10. Pour broth into small, individual five-ounce (150 ml) pitchers.

11. Serve each serving in a single serving bowl with an accompanying pitcher of broth.

12. To eat, show your child to squeeze the lime wedge over the bowl and set the used lime to the side. Then pour the broth over the top.

13. Serve with a soup spoon.

Bread

A feast for the senses!

I started making bread with my children from about the time they could stand at the counter. At first they would pour the pre-measured yeast or water into the bowl. Over time, with repetition and practice alongside me, they internalized the recipe and can now make a batch of dough from memory. We all learn as we take in sensorial experiences. Making bread pulls the whole child into the experience.

There is so much: the smell of yeast mixing with the warm water and sugar and the sight of the sponge the yeast forms; the sound of the sponge; the feel of the warm dough as you knead it; the smooth dome of dough after its first rise; and then the pull of resistance as you punch it down. As you knead the dough into a loaf again and enjoy the sight and smell of the full proof (a second rise), nothing can match the smell of fresh bread baking and then the taste of warm bread with melted butter. Your child experiences the chemistry of the ingredients, the connection to family as you work together, language enrichment as you discuss the process, and the mathematics of the measurements.

When we combine all of these experiences, your child is embraced in a family ritual that shapes his understanding of his world and human connection.

Bread

Makes two loaves

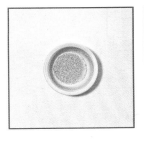    

Ingredients

1 tablespoon (9 g) active dry yeast

2 tablespoons (25 g) sugar

¼ cup (60 ml) olive oil, plus more for bowl

1 cup (250 ml) warm water

3 cups (360 g) all-purpose flour, plus extra for kneading

Materials

Small bowl for each ingredient

3 oz (90 ml) pitcher for oil

8 oz (250 ml) pitcher for water

Oil dispenser for oil for the bowl

Mixing bowl

Child-size wooden spoon

Rising bowl

Two loaf pans

Towel

Preparation

For this recipe, work side-by-side with your child for each step. See what he can do and let him do as much as possible on his own. After making this recipe together a few times, he will begin to internalize the steps and the timing and will become increasingly independent in making dough.

1. Pour the warm water into a large mixing bowl, sprinkle with yeast and sugar and let stand until foamy (about 5 minutes).

2. Add flour and stir until a sticky dough forms.

3. Add oil and mix well.

4. Turn onto floured surface, knead for five minutes.

5. Form dough into a ball.

6. Oil the inside of the bowl that will be used for rising.

7. Transfer dough to the oiled bowl and rub the top of dough ball with oil.

8. Cover the bowl with a towel and set aside in a warm, draft-free place until dough has doubled in bulk (about 1 hour).

9. After about an hour, remove the towel from the bowl and punch the dough down.

10. Turn the dough onto a floured surface and knead it for five minutes.

11. Divide the dough into two equal balls.

12. Form each ball of dough into a loaf shape and place in greased loaf pan. Cover the dough with a towel and set it aside in a warm, draft-free place until dough has doubled in volume (about 45 minutes).

13. Preheat oven to 375°F (190°C).

14. Bake at 375°F (190°C) for 30-35 minutes.

15. Remove and serve warm.

Cinnamon Rolls

Makes 8-10 servings

Once your child has started making dough, this is a fun recipe. It is based on the same dough from the bread recipe (p. 155). Instead of the second rise cycle, take the dough after the first rise and start this recipe.

Ingredients

Bread dough (p. 155)

2 tablespoons (25 g) sugar

1 teaspoon (2.5 g) cinnamon

2 tablespoons (30 g) unsalted butter, melted

Materials

Small bowl for each ingredient

Child-size rolling pin

Mixing bowl

Child-size rubber spatula

Child-size basting brush

A piece of thread

Greased 9" x 7" x 2" (23 x 18 x 5 cm) baking dish

IV. Recipes for Families

Preparation

1. Preheat oven to 350°F (175°C)

2. On a lightly floured surface, show your child how to use the rolling pin to roll out the dough into a thin rectangle. Push the rolling pin in the middle of the dough and roll out to the edge. Then repeat, starting in the middle and going the opposite direction. Invite your child to contuse rolling.

3. Show your child how to use the basting brush to brush the dough with melted butter. Invite your child to continue with the rest of the butter.

4. Ask you child to add the sugar to the cinnamon.

5. Show your child how to sprinkle the sugar mixture over the dough and invite your child to repeat. This takes practice to get the sugar distributed evenly, so do not worry of it is not perfect the first time you prepare the recipe :)

6. Start as one of the short ends of the triangle and slowly and tightly roll up the dough. Invite your child to roll with you.

7. Place the roll on your work surface with the seam-side down.

8. Put thread under roll about ¾" (2 cm) from one end. Cross thread above roll and pull tight, cutting a ¾" (2 cm) thick disc from the roll.

9. Move the thread 3/4" along the roll and invite your child to help you repeat the cutting movement with the thread. Continue until the roll is completely sliced into 3/4" discs.

10. Take turns placing each disc in greased baking dish, spiral side up.

11. Bake at 375°F (190°C) for 20 minutes, until lightly browned.

12. Remove and serve warm.

Recipes for Your Child To Prepare Independently

All of the recipes in this section are designed for your child to do independently. The first independent food preparation activities a young child can do include washing fruits and vegetables, peeling tangerines and bananas, and mixing a fruit salad. The skills they learn working alongside you help prepare them to independent in the kitchen. They learn to mix, chop pour, as well as taking time to add ingredients in order and checking the tray that all the ingredients are included. In this section, the first recipes are basic food preparation. The next few recipes are more advanced recipes, however, children who have experience in the kitchen are capable of completing them independently. You may find that your child asks for help with a step or two, and then is able to complete the rest on their own. You are the best person to determine which activities are best for your child; reading through these recipes will help you create your own simple food activities that are specific to your family culture.

In order to create an atmosphere for success in independent food preparation, it helps to demonstrate the task to your child the first time. Once your child has had a presentation from you, she may be able to repeat the activity independently. Many of these presentations may have already happened through your collaborative work in the kitchen. Some children need to see the activity more than once before they are ready to be independent. Once a child has had a lesson, they will do their best to recreate the movements and actions they observed. Remember: they will not repeat your movements exactly. They are still learning to control their hands and impulses, so their work will look different from yours. If you find that your child has drifted from the purpose of the activity, it may be that she needs a re-presentation from you or closer supervision while doing the activity.

Once your child is ready for independent food preparation, you can prepare the tray and place it out on the counter or a designated shelf for your child to choose. As your child gets older and more experienced in the kitchen, they can begin to prepare their won tray by gathering and measuring ingredients. Independent work does not mean unsupervised! See our section on Helping Versus Hovering (p. 44) for more guidance in this area.

A Note on Washing Dishes

Eventually, washing the dishes can be part of the food preparation (in order to leave the kitchen clean!). In the beginning of your child's experience with cooking, it is better to keep it as a separate activity.

Basic Recipes for Your Child To Prepare Independently

These recipes are designed to introduce beginning skills in preparing food. Your child may already have these skills from your collaborative work in the kitchen. You are the best judge of when to introduce these activities to your child. Children as young as 12 months are capable of repeating these recipes.

An adult should always supervise the use of tools and hot surfaces.

Sliced bananas

Corn On The Cob

Applesauce Cake

Using the Oven

It is up to you to know when your child is ready to use an oven. Many parents are comfortable with teaching their child to use a countertop convection or toaster oven, rather than a full oven. Always be present when your child is using an oven.

165

Sliced Bananas

Makes 1 serving

Ingredients

1 banana, prepared as below

Prepare the banana (by adult)

1. Cut off the ends

2. Slicing along the length only through the peel

3. Cut the banana in half, perpendicular to the slice you just made.

Materials

Cutting board

Bowl for banana

Bowl for banana slices

Round-tip cutting knife

Compost bowl

Preparation

1. Sit with your child at a low table.

2. Place the banana on the cutting board in front of you.

3. Show your child how to find where the peel is cut.

4. Find the edge and start to peel the banana.

5. Let your child finish peeling the banana.

6. Ask your child to place the banana on the cutting board.

7. Ask your child to place the peel in the compost bowl.

8. Show your child how to hold the knife properly.

9. Explain, "This is a knife and we only used for cutting food. We must always use it properly to keep everyone safe."

10. Cut one slice of banana.

11. Put the knife down and put the slice of banana in the proper bowl.

12. Repeat with another slice. Put the knife down each time.

13. Invite your child to finish slicing the banana.

14. When she has finished, ask her to take the peel to the compost and place the dishes in the dishwasher (or wherever you place dirty dishes)

15. Once you have cleaned up, ask your child to set the table for a snack.

16. Enjoy!

Corn on the Cob

Makes 4 servings

Ingredients

4 ears of corn

3 tablespoons (45 g) of butter

Materials

Tray for corn

Bowl for butter

Child-size spreading knife

Compost bin

Preparation

1. Show your child how to shuck the corn by removing each layer of leaves from the corn. Consider shucking the corn outside.

2. Place each leaf in the compost bin.

3. Repeat until you get to the silk.

4. Show your child how to carefully pull the silk off of the cob and place it in the compost bin.

5. Repeat until all the silk has been removed.

6. Show your child how to move your hand back and forth over the corn to remove the rest of the silk.

7. Steam the corn in a vegetable steamer or a pot of boiling water for 10 minutes. (This is a step for only the adult.)

8. Remove the corn from the pot or steamer and allow it to cool to the touch.

9. Show your child how to use the spreading knife to take a small amount of butter and run it along the kernels, pause to watch the butter melt and fall in-between the kernels.

10. Let your child repeat. When he is finished, place the corn on a serving plate and repeat with the other corn cobs

11. Once you have cleaned up, ask your child to set the table for snack.

12. Enjoy!

Applesauce Cake

Makes 6-8 servings

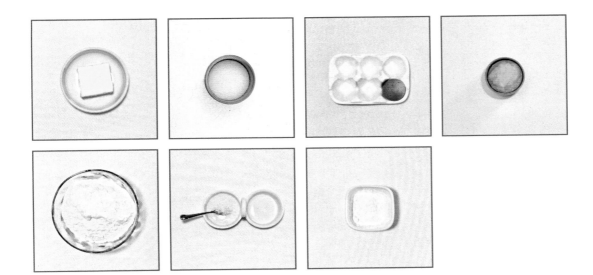

Ingredients

⅛ cup (30 g) butter, softened

⅛ cup (25 g) sugar

1 egg

¼ cup (60 ml, about 60 g) applesauce

½ cup (60 g) all-purpose flour

A pinch of salt

¼ tablespoon (3.5 g) baking powder

Materials

Small bowl for each ingredient

Mixing bowl

Hand mixer

Child-size rubber spatula

Greased mini Bundt pan

Powdered sugar shaker

Preparation

1. Preheat oven to 350°F (175°C).

2. Using the hand mixer, cream butter and sugar in the mixing bowl.

3. Mix in egg and applesauce (adult may need to help with adding the egg if your child is new to cracking eggs). Then both you and your child wash your hands. (It is good practice to create a habit of washing hands after touching raw egg.)

4. Add the remaining ingredients. Mix well.

5. Pour batter into the greased Bundt pan. Use a spatula to scrape mixing bowl and get all the batter into the pan.

6. Place pan in preheated oven. (Adult does this part.)

7. Bake for 20-25 minutes, or until cake starts to pull away from the sides and the top is golden brown.

8. Remove from the oven.

9. Allow the pan to cool to the touch. Place the serving plate, up side down on top of the cake. Turn the cake pan and plate at the same time, transferring the cake to the plate.

10. Sprinkle the top of the cake with powdered sugar.

11. Serve warm.

Advanced Recipes for Your Child To Prepare Independently

Once your child has mastered slicing, mixing, pouring skills, and understands the process of adding each ingredient of a recipe, they can move to more complex recipes. This section has recipes that have more ingredients and more steps and can be repeated by children as young as 18 months if the tray is prepared. The new skill for an older child is measuring the ingredients and, later, reading the recipe. The first time you introduce a recipe, stay alongside your child during their work. Allow your child to be as independent as possible.

Once your child understands to do one step at a time and to measure carefully, they can be independent with the recipes. Note that their efforts might not come out just right or even edible! Be understanding. In our house, we have had a number of recipes that we consider just a learning experience. Sometimes they miss measure or forget an ingredient completely. They soon learn that these mistakes change the taste, texture, and look of the food. All are important lessons in cooking, and often best learned through experience. Help your children to reflect and find their errors. Making mistakes is human! It's how we all learn.

An adult should always supervise the use of tools and hot surfaces.

Guacamole

Sweet Potato Muffins

Lemon Lavender Shortbread

Ranch Potato bake

Pear tart

Guacamole

Makes 6-8 servings

Ingredients

1 avocado, cut in half

2 tablespoons (7 g) cilantro

Pinch of salt

½ lime

½ tomato, chopped

Materials

Small bowl for each ingredient

Child-size spoon

Juicer

Child-size masher

Mixing bowl

Compost bowl

Preparation

1. Use a large spoon to scoop the avocado into the bowl.

2. Use fingers to tear cilantro into the bowl.

3. Place stems in compost bowl.

4. Add a pinch of salt.

5. Juice the half lime and pour the juice into the bowl.

6. Add the chopped tomato to bowl.

7. Mash with the masher.

8. Serve with tortilla chips.

Sweet Potato Muffins

Makes 8-10 servings

  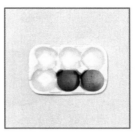  

Ingredients

½ cup (100 g) sugar

½ cup (125 ml) coconut oil

2 eggs

1 ¾ cups (210 g) all-purpose flour

1 teaspoon (6 g) baking soda

½ teaspoon (3 g) salt

½ teaspoon (2 g) ground cinnamon

½ teaspoon (1 g) ground nutmeg

⅓ cup (80 ml) water

2 sweet potatoes; cooked, peeled, and mashed

Materials

Small bowl for each ingredient

Hand mixer

Mixing bowl

⅓ cup (80 ml) pitcher for water

½ cup (125 ml) pitcher for oil

Mini muffin pan

Child-size spoon

Non-stick spray or muffin pan lines

Preparation

1. Preheat oven to 350°F (175°C).

2. Spray mini muffin cups with non-stick spray or line with paper liners and set aside.

3. Combine sugar and oil in a mixing bowl and mix well.

4. Add eggs and beat.

5. Add flour, baking soda, salt, cinnamon, and nutmeg. Mix well.

6. Add water. Mix well.

7. Stir in the mashed sweet potatoes. Stir until all the ingredients are mixed well.

8. Spoon the batter into the mini muffin cups until they are each half full.

9. Bake at 350°F (175°C) for 12-15 minutes.

10. Remove and serve warm.

Limited Space

When setting up your tray, you may find some recipes require many ingredients. I have found it helpful to combine some ingredients into a single bowl in order to simplify. For example; baking soda and salt or cinnamon and nutmeg.

Lemon Lavender Shortbread

Makes 10-12 servings

Ingredients

¼ cup (60 ml) sugar

1 teaspoon (1 g) dried lavender blossoms, chopped

1 teaspoon (5 ml or about 2 g) lemon zest

8 tablespoons (120 g) unsalted butter, softened

1 cup all-purpose flour (120 g)

½ teaspoon (2.5 g) salt

Materials

Child-size grater

Pastry cutter

Child-size spatula

Small bowl for each ingredient

Mixing bowl

Child-size rolling pin

Cookie cutters

Baking sheet lined with parchment paper

Preparation

1. Preheat the oven to 350° (175°C).

2. Mix the sugar with the chopped lavender and lemon zest in mixing bowl.

3. Cut in the butter with the pastry cutter.

4. Add the flour and salt. Mix with spatula.

5. Place dough onto floured surface and roll out ¼" (5mm) thick with the rolling pin.

6. Cut shapes with cookie cutters.

7. Place shapes on the baking sheet lined with parchment paper.

8. Bake shortbread at 350° (175°C) for 20 to 25 minutes.

Ranch Potato Bake

Makes 8-10 servings

Ingredients

2 russet potatoes, peeled, baked, and sliced

1/2 teaspoon (2 ml) salt

1/4 teaspoon (1 ml) ground black pepper

3 tablespoons (45 ml) butter, cubed

4 ounces (115 g) shredded Colby-Monterey Jack cheese

4 ounces (120 ml) Ranch dressing

Materials

Measuring spoons

Mixing bowl

Small bowl for each ingredient

Child-size spatula

4 ounce (120 ml) pitcher for ranch dressing

9" x 7" x 2" (23 x 18 x 5 cm) baking dish

Aluminum foil

Preparation

1. Preheat oven to 400 °F (205°C).

2. Lightly grease the inside of the baking dish.

3. In mixing bowl, mix potatoes with salt and pepper.

4. Add ranch and shredded cheese. Mix well.

5. Scoop into prepared baking dish.

6. Cover baking dish with aluminum foil.

7. Bake at 400 °F (205°C) for 12 minutes

8. Remove foil and bake five more minutes until cheese is melted and bubbly.

9. Remove and serve warm.

Pear Tart

Makes four servings

Ingredients

5 shortbread cookies - crushed

¼ cup (30 g) all-purpose flour

3 tablespoons (45 g) unsalted butter, melted

1 tablespoon (12 g) brown sugar

½ teaspoon (2 g) sugar

½ teaspoon (2.5 ml) pure vanilla extract

¼ teaspoon (1 g) ground cinnamon

2 pears, cored and sliced

Materials

Small bowl for each ingredient

Cutting board

Child-size serrated knife

Mixing bowl

Child size wooden spoon

Mini tart pan

Preparation

1. Preheat oven to 350 °F (175°C).

2. In mixing bowl, combine crushed shortbread cookies, flour, and 2 tablespoons (30 g) melted butter.

3. Pat mixture into bottom and up the sides of tart pan.

4. Bake at 350 °F (175°C) for 10 minutes. Set aside.

5. Preheat oven to 400 °F (205°C).

6. In mixing bowl, combine the one tablespoon (15 g) of melted butter, with brown sugar, sugar, vanilla extract, and cinnamon. Mix well.

7. Add sliced pears and mix until pears are covered with sugar mixture.

8. Place pears in a single layer on the tart crust in the pan.

9. Bake at 400 °F (205°C) for 12 minutes.

10. Remove and let cool for at least 10 minutes before eating.

— Part V —
Frequently Asked Questions

Frequently Asked Questions

For the past twenty years, I have been cooking with children: my children, my friend's children, nieces and nephews, and children in schools where I have worked. When I opened Studio June, I knew baking and cooking would be a core part of the children's experiences in classes. Later, when I began Family Friendly Home, my in-home consultation work, I began helping parents set up their kitchens and dining rooms to support their children's activities at home.

Rarely is there a child who doesn't love to cook! Even the children who don't like to eat, like to cook. Why? Cooking has purpose. It also requires focus and develops eye-hand coordination. Parents I work with see these skills develop firsthand and then bring these activities into their homes. I have compiled a list of the questions I get most frequently from parents at Studio June and in my work with clients at Family Friendly Home. I hope this Q&A section will support you in your journey to enjoying the time you spend in the kitchen with your own children.

What do I do if my child throws food?

This is a sure sign your child is not focused on eating. He may not be hungry enough to eat, so it is a good time to help him away from the table for a while. Let him know that when he is hungry enough to sit and eat, you will offer his meal again. Offer the food again after about 30 minutes. If he is hungry he will eat. If he is testing you, it is important to repeat putting the food away. This is a way that he tests the rules to see what the outcome is. When you consistently respond in the same way, he learns to understand and trust the rule.

What do we do about snacks on the go?

It is healthiest to pre-make snacks and have them in the fridge or pantry at home. Using small containers with easy-snap lids such as the "bento box" by Think Baby, you can create pre-measured snacks of carrot sticks, cheese cubes, fruit slices, or bread with sun butter. These are all quick and healthful choices when you are away from home. Pre-packaged, store-bought snacks are not the most nutritious; they are often heavily processed and have preservatives, as well as high levels of sodium, sugar or artificial flavors, and dyes. In recent years it has become popular to use pouch-style snacks that are meant to be sucked. In addition to the contents being so heavily processed, the pouch snack is an unfortunate development as it teaches children to suck, as infants do, rather than progressing their chewing skills. Pouch snacks also contribute to limiting opportunities for strengthening hand skills with the pincer grasp. Lastly, pouch-style snacks are puréed and do not allow children to advance their appreciation of textured food and may even lead them to reject solid food that must be chewed, making the transition to eating healthful meals longer and more difficult.

What kind of knife is safe for my child?

The safest knife is the correct knife for the job. If spreading, a child should be offered a rounded tip spreading knife or small table knife. If cutting fruits and vegetables, a wavy chopping knife or a serrated acrylic knife are the best for the job. Always demonstrate how to handle and use a knife before letting your child use it. Supervise closely when your child uses a knife; have patience as he learns to use it safely. Parents often want to jump in too soon. If your child misuses the knife, it may be best to put it away and demonstrate again on another day.

Why do you use breakable dishes, even for infants and young children?

There are many reasons why we use glass and ceramic dishes. The most important and significant one is that children are capable of using these items and giving them plastic or metal is not necessary. Like the use of a 'sippy cup', it is not needed and only stands in the way of children learning how to handle breakable items with care and how to clean up if one is dropped.

Eating off of plastic or metal is not as pleasant of an experience. Additionally, plastic leaches chemicals into food, and serving food from metal can change the flavor. Ceramic plates are the best for serving food and therefore children deserve the opportunity to learn to eat from ceramic dishes from the first meal.

Where do I get real dishes and silverware that is the right size?

Online retailers sell "young children's forks and spoons" which are perfect for children six months to three years old. "Child-size" flatware is best for children between three and six years old.

Appetizer plates are the perfect size for meals for children six months to three years old. The same plates can be used for snacks for children between three and six years old. As a child starts to eat more food in one sitting, salad plates are a perfect size. Choose a plate with a small rim, as it can be helpful when scooping or spearing food. See more about sizing by age on page 54

Why does my child drop the spoon after each bite?

When children start eating solid foods, at about six months old, they are still working on eye-hand coordination and may not yet have mastered *intentional release*, which comes at around seven months. *Intentional release* is a child's ability to consistently send a message from their brain to their hand to let go of what they are holding. At the time that a child starts solid food, he may not yet have this ability; it may appear that he throws his spoon after each bite. It will take time and practice. Also, some children, once they have acquired this skill, like to practice releasing every chance they get. This is often seen as a game between child and adult and you may find yourself picking something up repeatedly! Try to not make it a game and just pick up the spoon and move on without drawing too much attention to it.

My child does not seem to want to eat. Why is he refusing food?

There is no one reason that children might refuse food. It is important to take note of the many aspects of your child's life in order to figure out why he won't eat. If he once used to eat many foods and now he seems to refuse most foods except a few, (or he refuses all foods) notice if something in his life has changed.

Here are some reasons his eating pattern may have changed:

1. He is not hungry right now.

2. He is more interested in something else that is happening at this moment.

3. He does not feel well (getting sick or overtired).

4. Food is not appetizing for him (gets stomach aches when eating or he has some texture aversions).

5. His routine has changed and he feels a lack of control in his life. New school? New caregiver? New house? Parent(s) had a change in their routine? This can be remedied by inviting your child to have more participation in choices, e.g., what to wear or whether to go to the park or the pool. Children who feel their life is constantly controlled by others may respond by taking control whenever possible, and that includes refusing to eat.

6. You may have fallen into a routine yourself, where you only prepare his favorite foods because you know he will eat them, and when you prepare something new, he refuses. This is a good point to check in with the variety of foods you eat with your child and are offering routinely.

7. He is testing his ability to say "no". He may be trying out the word "no" and learning the power it has.

Whatever the reason your child is refusing to eat, it is important to have patience and stay consistent. Continue to offer healthful and varied choices at regular and routine times.

If you are concerned about your child's nutrition, take notes about what and how much food your child is eating each day and discuss with your pediatrician.

Can I purchase a set of furniture that he will grow into?

Although some companies make tables that are marketed as "grow with me," these are not always the best tables to invest in. A young child needs a sturdy, low table where he can sit with proper posture and have his feet flat on the floor. This helps with limiting wiggles and swinging feet while at the table. In my experience, it is best to purchase a table and chair suitable for six months old to two years old and then a new table for two and a half to six years old. See page 51 for more information about choosing furniture.

How do I teach my child to drink from an open glass?

Start with an open glass at the first weaning meal (about six months old). Use a small 2 oz. (60 ml) glass; put a small amount of water in it. Offer it to your child to hold and with her two hands on the glass, help her put the glass to her mouth and tip it up. When she is finished, help her to carefully place it back down on the table. Repeat this as she is interested.

What can I do when my young child keeps walking away from the table in the middle of a meal?

It is important to teach your child that he must sit while eating. Only offer food when he is seated at the table. If he walks away, let him know that you are going to put his meal away for later. If he returns to the table right away, let him continue with his meal. If he continues to get up from his chair and you feel you are caught in a game, simply remove his food and say, "You must not be hungry enough to sit and eat. I will put your food away until later." Re-offer the same food after 30 minutes or so. Doing this helps him to understand that the rule is firm and that food is available when he sits at the table. He will eat if he is hungry. He is learning to balance his urges to move with his need to eat. Know that you will not starve him, and that you are being clear about your expectations. Do the same with liquids. 'Sippy cups' suggest that it is okay to walk around with a beverage. (read more about 'sippy cups' on page 21) The safest way to drink and save your house from spills is to stay seated. Keeping food at the table is your best chance to not get it all over your couch!

My child does not seem to eat enough. How can I get him to eat more?

It is important to recognize when your child is hungry. It is also important to recognize how much food your child needs vs. how much you think is 'enough'. Children need different amounts of food at different times of development. This is why we teach them to respond to their body cues from early on (see page 77).

Some children love to eat, while others rarely slow down to take a bite. In order to make sure your child is offered enough food:

1. **Always offer healthful, whole meals and snacks and stay away from foods with high sugar content or that are heavily processed.** If you always offer healthful food options, you will know that your child is eating for health when he eats.

2. **Offer food at regular times** (breakfast, lunch, and dinner)

3. **Minimize distractions during meal time**. Do not have other noises or activities happening in the same space as the meal. This will help your child to focus on the activity at hand—eating—and not want to leave to be part of another activity. It is also important not to distract your child during meal time by putting him in front of a video (movie) or screen. Make eating the activity.

4. **Eat with your child.** Children often want to be a part of what you are doing. If you expect him to sit and eat, it can help to model the behavior and make it an enjoyable activity for both of you.

5. **Don't mind the mess.** Try not to clean the table, floor, or your child (!) during meals. Save that for after the meal. Each time you leave to pick something up, you model the behavior of getting up during a meal.

Notes

1 https://www.nichd.nih.gov/health/topics/breastfeeding/conditioninfo/recommendations. American Academy of Pediatrics. (2012). Breastfeeding and the use of human milk. Pediatrics, 129(3), e827–e841. Retrieved April 27, 2012, from http://pediatrics.aappublications.org/content/129/3/e827.full.pdf+html

2 https://thefamilydinnerproject.org/about-us/benefits-of-family-dinners

3 https://www.ted.com/talks/julie_lythcott_haims_how_to_raise_successful_kids_without_over_parenting

4 https://www.choosemyplate.gov/protein-foods

5 https://www.choosemyplate.gov/protein-foods

6 https://www.cdc.gov/nutrition/infantandtoddlernutrition/mealtime/signs-your-child-is-hungry-or-full.html

Sarah Moudry

Sarah Moudry is the founder of Studio June and Family Friendly Home. She brings her passion for supporting young families to a greater audience. A longtime advocate for Montessori education, Sarah is AMI Montessori trained at both the Primary and Assistance to Infancy levels and has worked with children ranging in age from newborns to 14-year-olds. She consults with teachers and parents on creating home and school environments for children combining education and design principles. An authority on pregnancy, childbirth, toileting, and other early childhood development topics, Sarah Moudry speaks regularly at educational conferences worldwide and is the author of several books and videos on early childhood education.

Also Published

Toilet Awareness - Second Edition (2019)
Aprendiendo a Usar el Inodoro (2015)
Toilet Awareness - First Edition (2012)
What Is the Montessori Toddler Community (2008)
In a Montessori Home (2008)
Aid to Life (2011; contributor)

Resources

www.studiojune.com
www.familyfriendlyhome.com
www.toiletawareness.com
www.firstfoodstofamilymeals.com

Made in United States
North Haven, CT
23 October 2021